3

ts

Introduction

4

Introduction

Britain and London Visitor Centre
1 Regent St, London SW1Y 4XT
E-mail: bvlcinfo@visitbritain.org
visitbritain.com

London needs little introduction. It is a city of contrasts – known on the one hand as a cradle of contemporary culture and innovation, and on the other as a city that lives and breathes history, complete with ancient traditions and long-standing institutions.

London is Europe's largest metropolis by far, and a trend-setter among world cities, continually reinventing itself with the times, absorbing people and steering cultural movements. Free-spirited, proud, unique – London has something for everyone, then a bit more.

Cityscape

With the exception of Canary Wharf, London is a low-rise city, extending outwards for many miles along the banks of the River Thames and knitted together by what is essentially a collection of villages, each with their own unique character. Striking modern architecture stands alongside the great churches of Sir Christopher Wren, while elegant Georgian squares, expansive parklands and riverside footpaths provide welcome respite from city life. With its medieval tangle of streets, London is a wonderful place to amble aimlessly, making discoveries at every turn.

Landmarks

From ground-breaking exhibition spaces to characterful heritage pieces London has more than its fair share of famous landmarks. The great globe of St Paul's Cathedral glows golden in the evening sun, as does the circular thatched roof of the Globe Theatre, a faithful reproduction of the original theatre in which Shakespeare himself performed. Striking contemporary landmarks include Tate Modern and the London Eye – respectively the largest art gallery and observation wheel in the world. Both have quickly installed themselves in the nation's affections. Then of course there are the timeless sights of Westminster Abbey, the Houses of Parliament, the Tower of London, Big Ben, Greenwich and Buckingham Palace.

Introduction

London Visitor Centre, Waterloo Arrivals Hall,
Waterloo International, London SE1 7LT
E-mail: london.visitorcentre@iceplc.com
T: 020 7620 1550

Museums and galleries

Few cities in the world can compete with London when it comes to museums and galleries. There's enough to keep you going for a year (let alone a long weekend), from one of the largest museums in the world, the British Museum, to what is fast becoming the world's most popular art gallery, Tate Modern – and dozens more in between. The 'Museum Mile' is a great place to start, linking 18 of London's museums and galleries between the River Thames and Euston.

Eating out

In 2005, London dominated the list of 50 Best Restaurants in the World, compiled by the influential *Restaurant Magazine*. It's an indication of the great strides the city has made towards becoming the gourmet capital of the world. If you want the best of the best, across world cuisines, you'll do very nicely in London. Thanks to the city's wide cultural diversity, the range of food on offer across the budgets is simply staggering. Whatever tickles your fancy, you'll find it in London.

Shopping

It need hardly be said that London and shopping go hand in hand. The city has always been a magnet for shoppers, many of whom cross continents for the privilege. Start with the markets – Portobello, Camden, Covent Garden or Spitalfields; then move on to some of London's great shopping institutions – the boutiques of Bond Street; the tailors of Savile Row; and the luxury department stores of Harrods, Libertys, Selfridges and Fortnum & Mason. It's impossible to leave London empty-handed in any way.

6

British Airways London Eye

Designed as one of the city's millennium projects, the British Airways London Eye has now become Britain's most popular paying tourist attraction. A striking addition to the London skyline, 'the Wheel' offers the best way to get a bird's-eye view of the metropolis.

▨ Jubilee Gardens, South Bank
T 0870 500 0600 (ticket hotline)
✆ Westminster or Waterloo
➾ Waterloo

✷ Daily, Oct–May 10–8; Jun–Sept 10–9 (ticket office open 9.30). Closed part of Jan for annual maintenance
ba-londoneye.com

The high life

A half-hour trip on the world's highest Ferris wheel will make your spirits soar. The Eye provides a matchless panorama of the city, especially on a fine day, of course. From its position on the south bank of the Thames, many famous London landmarks are visible. However, those nervous about heights or claustrophobia need not worry as the wheel moves slowly, while the capsules are enclosed and spacious.

The sky's the limit

Because the mainly glass capsules are on the outside of the wheel, there are completely open views of the city, and even beyond. On a clear day you can see up to 25 miles (40km) away, as far as St Albans Cathedral, north of London. Sunsets can be spectacular, while if you visit after dark you will enjoy seeing buildings such as the Houses of Parliament and St Paul's Cathedral lit up in dramatic style.

High tech

Designed by Marks Barfield Associates, the 134-metre (440-foot) diameter wheel astonishingly works on the same principles as an ordinary bicycle wheel. However, cutting-edge technology was used to insert a solar cell in each of the 32 capsules, which helps power ventilation, lighting and communication.

Advance booking

At peak times, it is essential to book ahead, either by phone or in person. Nonetheless, even with pre-booked tickets you may have to queue for some time before you can get on the wheel, but the wait is well worth it.

★ Highlights
Great views across London

ℹ Information
🍽 Cafes in nearby County Hall
♿ Excellent
£ Expensive

world's highest Ferris wheel

British Museum

The British Museum contains one of the greatest collections of antiquities in the world. More than six million objects from many different civilizations and cultures are on view in Britain's largest museum.

🛈 **Great Russell Street, WC1**
(another entrance in Montague St)

T 020 7323 8000

🚇 Holborn, Tottenham Court Road or Russell Square

🏛 **Museum** Sat–Wed 10–5.30;
Thurs, Fri 10–8.30
Great Court Sun–Wed 9–6;
Thurs–Sat 9am–11pm

thebritishmuseum.ac.uk

Origins

The story of the British Museum began when Sir Hans Sloane died in 1753, leaving his collection of about 70,000 artefacts to the nation. This was given a permanent home in 1759 when Britain's first public museum opened in a 17th-century mansion.

Expansion

Sloane's original collection was later complemented by the splendid bequests from Kings George II, III and IV, as well as other monarchs, not to mention the Townley bequest and the Elgin Marbles (sculptures of the Parthenon). To accommodate these cultural riches, Robert Smirke designed a magnificent new museum in the neoclassical style, which was completed by his brother Sydney in 1857. However, because the spoils of expeditions and excavations around the British Empire continued to expand the collection, the Natural History division moved to South Kensington (see page 26).

The Great Court

After the British Library relocated to St Pancras in 1998, the Great Court was redeveloped by the celebrated architect Sir Norman Foster, with a spectacular glass roof, making this London's largest covered public square. The circular Reading Room at its hub has been restored and is now open to the general public for the first time. In addition, the Sainsbury Galleries were built for the African collections. Today five million people visit the museum every year to look at the treasures of two million years of human history.

★ Highlights
Oriental antiquities
Sainsbury Galleries
Rosetta Stone
Current prints and drawings
Islamic art
Mildenhall and Sutton Hoo treasures
Elgin Marbles
Assyrian and Egyptian rooms
Roman Britain Gallery
Great Court

🛈 Information	
🍽	Restaurant, cafes
♿	Very good
£	Free except for some temporary exhibitions, tours and late openings
+	Full educational programme

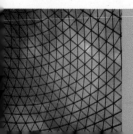

Britain's
first public
museum

10

Buckingham Palace

Although bought by King George III in 1761, Buckingham Palace only became the official royal residence in 1837, at the beginning of the reign of Queen Victoria. The exterior is harmonious, if somewhat plain, for a palace, but the interiors are truly magnificent, mainly due to the Regency architect John Nash, who doubled the palace's size on behalf of the extravagant George IV.

🚇 The Mall SW1
State Rooms **T** 020 7766 7300
Queen's Gallery **T** 020 7766 7301
Royal Mews **T** 020 7766 7302

⊖ Victoria, St James's Park or Green Park
≋ Victoria
royal.gov.uk

State Rooms
The State Rooms were first opened to the public in 1993 to raise funds for the rebuilding of the fire-ravaged Windsor Castle. The rooms are used for state occasions, and are only open to the public during August and September, when the Royal Family are staying at their summer residence.

Queen's Gallery
The Queen's private art collection – the greatest in the world – displays paintings, drawings and furniture, including works by Canaletto, Rembrandt and Rubens, as well as watercolours by Queen Victoria. The works exhibited are changed every six months.

Royal Mews
The royal stables house the state carriages and coaches, some of which were used for the Queen's Golden Jubilee celebrations in 2002. They include the ornate Gold Carriage (for coronations), the Glass State Coach (for foreign dignitaries and ambassadors) and the open-topped landau, which was used for the weddings of the Prince of Wales in 1981 and the Duke of York in 1986.

Changing the Guard
May–July 11.30am (rest of year on alternate days weather permitting – call to check).

★ Highlights
Throne Room
Table of Grand Commanders, Blue Drawing Room
Secret royal door in the White Drawing Room
Liveried beadles in the Queen's Gallery
State Coach, Royal Mews
Changing the Guard

i Information	
♿	Excellent
£	Palace expensive; Gallery and Mews moderate; Changing the Guard free
+	No photography

greatest private art collection

12 Houses of Parliament and Big Ben

The Houses of Parliament is not only the seat of British government but also one of the oldest representative assemblies in the world. And to many, the imposing clock tower with its massive hourly bell, known as Big Ben, is the symbol of London.

🚇 **Westminster SW1**
T 020 7219 3000
⊖ Westminster
⇌ Waterloo or Victoria

Tours during summer recess (beg of Aug to late Sept) 9.30–5; during session on Mon, Tues and Wed mornings, and Fri (afternoons) for UK residents only. Call 0870 906 3773 to confirm details.

parliament.uk

Crown and state

The Houses of Parliament are located on the site of the Palace of Westminster, which was the principal residence of kings from the mid-11th century until 1512. William the Conqueror chose Westminster as the place to keep an eye on the London merchants. It later became the centre of government for England, then Britain, then a world empire.

Mother of parliaments

Here the foundations of Parliament were laid according to Edward I's Model Parliament of 1295. This evolved into a lower house, the House of Commons (elected Members of Parliament), and an upper house, the House of Lords (unelected senior members of State and Church). Henry VIII's Reformation Parliament of 1529–36 ended Church domination of Parliament and made the Commons more powerful than the Lords. But it wasn't until after the Glorious Revolution of 1688 that the authority of Parliament over the King was established.

Centre of an empire

Having survived the Catholic conspiracy to blow up Parliament (on 5 November 1605, Guy Fawkes Night), all the medieval buildings were destroyed by a fire in 1834, except for Westminster Hall. Phoenix-like, Charles Barry's plans and AW Pugin's detailed design together created a masterpiece of Victorian Gothic to rise above the ashes.

★ Highlights

Statue of Oliver Cromwell

Big Ben

Commons or Lords debates

St Stephen's Hall

Westminster Hall

Jewel Tower

ℹ Information

£ Parliament free (UK residents should apply to their MP; non-UK residents can apply for tickets to their embassy or consulate.)
Tours expensive
Jewel Tower inexpensive

+ State Opening of Parliament mid-Nov

principal residence of kings

14

Imperial War Museum

Founded in 1917, the Imperial War Museum shows the impact of war on soldiers and civilians in Britain and the Commonwealth since World War I. The fact that this building was previously the Bethlehem Hospital for the Insane (known as 'Bedlam') somehow seems appropriate for a museum that reveals the madness of war, as well the suffering and courage of those involved.

🏛 **Lambeth Road SE1**
T 020 7416 5320
⊖ Lambeth North

≊ Waterloo
❀ Daily 10–6
iwm.org.uk

Twentieth-century war

The Large Exhibits Gallery contains huge weapons and vehicles from war in the 20th century, including guns, tanks and aircraft. The First World War Galleries include a re-creation of a trench on the Somme, with convincing lighting, sound and smell effects. The Second World War Galleries feature the multi-sensory Blitz Experience, which reconstructs an air-raid shelter and blitzed street from the bombed London of 1940.

Galleries of war

The permanent Holocaust Exhibition examines the genocide of European Jews and other minority groups before and during World War II, using original documents and objects to show the horror of what happened

(not suitable for younger children). Other galleries include Conflicts Since 1945, the Victoria Cross and George Cross Gallery, Field Marshal Montgomery and Secret War (which looks at the clandestine operations of the British Secret Services).

War art

The top floor houses the museum's art collection, including works by CRW Nevinson, Stanley Spencer, John Nash, John Piper (both world wars), Peter Howson (Bosnia) and John Keane (the first Gulf War), many of which were commissioned by the museum itself. The museum also houses John Singer Sargent's large and nightmarish picture of 1918–19, simply entitled *Gassed*, a graphic depiction of chemical warfare.

★ Highlights

Trench on the Somme
Blitz Experience
Holocaust Exhibition
Gassed, John Singer Sargent

i Information

🍴	Cafe
♿	Excellent
£	Free
+	Special exhibitions, talks, films, full education programme

16

Kensington Palace

Bought by William III as a healthier place to live than the dank Whitehall Palace (which made his asthma worse), Kensington Palace continued to be a home for sovereigns until the death of George II in 1760. Since then it has been inhabited by various other members of the Royal Family, including the late Princess Diana.

⧉ Kensington Gardens w8
T 0870 751 5170
⊖ High Street Kensington
or Queensway

⚜ Daily, Mar–Oct 10–6;
Nov–Feb 10–5
royal.gov.uk

Location, location, location

In 1689, a year after he was crowned, William and his wife Mary bought a Jacobean mansion in the village of Kensington, the ideal location to combine London socialising with country living. Architects Sir Christopher Wren and Nicholas Hawksmoor were brought in to extend and improve the house as befitted a royal residence.

Palatial grandeur

The next monarch, Queen Anne, built an Orangery (with woodcarvings by the master craftsman Grinling Gibbons). Although the rooms were relatively small, George I helped to introduce the majesty of a palace with the addition of Colen Campbell's staircase and state rooms, gracefully decorated by William Kent. Not only

the house itself but also the gardens expanded as some of the adjoining royal Hyde Park was appended by George II's wife, Queen Caroline (see Kensington Gardens on page 34).

A home for princesses

Princess Victoria was born in the palace in 1819, and was baptised in the splendid Cupola Room. She lived here until she became Queen in 1837, and later opened her childhood home to the public. Memorabilia from her time in the palace can be seen in the Victorian Rooms. Over a hundred years later, Diana, Princess of Wales took up residence here. There is a permanent exhibition about her in the palace.

★ Highlights
King's Grand Staircase
Presence Chamber
Wind dial in the King's Gallery
King's Drawing Room
Princess Victoria's dolls' house
Royal Ceremonial Dress Collection
Princess Diana Dress Collection
Italian Gardens

i Information
🍽 Cafe in the Orangery
♿ Few
£ Expensive; family tickets
+ Guided tour every 30 minutes

18

London Zoo

When London Zoo opened, it was intended to be a purely scientific institution, dedicated to the study of animals. Later it became a highly popular tourist attraction, with more than three million visitors a year. Today a balance has been struck, so that study and conservation take place alongside display and entertainment, with the zoo very conscious of its responsibility to protect endangered species.

∎ Regent's Park NW1
T 020 7722 3333
⊖ Camden Town
⇌ Euston

❋ Daily, Mar–Oct 10–5.30;
Nov–Feb 10–4
londonzoo.co.uk

Exotic animals in London
In 1826 Sir Stamford Raffles, the founder of Singapore Colony, established the Zoological Society of London with the scientist and inventor Sir Humphry Davy. The idea was to facilitate the study of exotic animals by scientists. It was not until 1847 that the zoo was fully open to the general public. The society's own collection of exotic animals – zebras, monkeys, kangaroos and bears – was soon enlarged by the royal menageries from Windsor Castle and the royal zoo from the Tower of London.

Animal kingdom
Over the years new arrivals included chimpanzees, giraffes and elephants. The world's first reptile house, aquarium and insect houses were built. Today there are 14.5 hectares (36 acres) containing about 5,000 animals in three areas of gardens linked by tunnels and bridges.

A zoo for modern times
Aware of the global controversy over zoos, London Zoo now emphasises conservation and education. It houses the Institute of Zoology, which carries out research and funds important groundbreaking fieldwork. The Children's Zoo shows children how to care for pets. B.U.G.S! (Biodiversity Underpinning Global Survival) explores the conservation of biological diversity.

Credit: London Zoo

★ Highlights
Big cats

Children's Zoo pet care centre

Lord Snowdon's aviaries

Reversed lighting to see nocturnal mammals

Chimpanzees

B.U.G.S!

i Information
❘❂❘ Restaurants, cafes and kiosks

ᯓ Good

£ Very expensive

+ Lectures, talks, regular animal feeding times; Animals in Action programme; animal adoption schemes

Madame Tussauds

See how many famous (and infamous) people you can identify at Madame Tussauds' waxworks collection, from Shakespeare to Madonna. Highlights include new interactive exhibitions, the Chamber of Horrors and The Stardome.

🄵 **Marylebone Road w1**
T 0870 919 0046
⊖ Baker Street or Marylebone

❀ Mon–Fri 9.30–5.30;
Sat, Sun 9–6
madame-tussauds.co.uk

Madame Tussauds

Madame Tussaud lived in Paris during the French Revolution and learnt the art of waxworks from her uncle. In 1802 she brought her collection to London, which included the guillotine blade that beheaded Marie Antoinette (in Chamber Live, together with many models of the infamous). It is said that Madame Tussauds is a barometer of celebrity: if you've been measured up for a wax model, then you've 'made it'; but if you've been taken out, then your star is on the wane. Visitors supply ideas for new inclusions. There are themed areas such as Divas (the likes of Britney, Kylie and Beyoncé) and Warriors, a battle between Alexander the Great and Achilles, using live combat and digital technology. The dark-ride finale, called the Spirit of London, takes you on a journey through history.

Get interactive

Blush, London's hottest venue for mingling with the world's most famous celebrities, invites you to get up-close and personal with some of Hollywood's biggest stars. Join the glamorous party along with the likes of Brad Pitt, J Lo and Colin Farrell. Plus, Johnny Depp leads his pirates (and you) into the hull of the Black Pearl, or you may prefer to spill your feelings in the interactive Big Brother diary room.

The Stardome

Housed in the original Planetarium building, The Stardome presents The Wonderful World of Stars, a quirky animated look at the world of celebrity from the perspective of endearing aliens.

★ Highlights
Kylie
Blush
Pirates of the Caribbean
Chamber Live
Big Brother diary room
The Stardome.

ℹ Information	
🍽	Cafes
♿	Very good
£	Very expensive

22

National Gallery

From relatively humble beginnings, the National Gallery has developed into one of the world's greatest art collections. As the national collection of Western European painting, all major schools of painting and the most renowned painters are represented, with works of art dating from 1250 to 1900.

▣ Trafalgar Square WC2
T 020 7747 2885
Ө Charing Cross or Leicester Square
⇌ Charing Cross

∰ Mon, Tues, Thurs–Sun 10–6; Wed 10–9. Late openings for some special exhibitions
nationalgallery.org.uk

Overview
Founded in 1824 with only 38 pictures, the National Gallery now has over 2,000 artworks. Displayed in William Wilkins's neoclassical building and the Sainsbury Wing extension, they provide a magnificent overview of European painting, from Giotto to Cézanne.

Development
The origins of the collection, unusually for a national collection, are not royal but from the bequest of John Julius Angerstein, a self-made financier. The directors of the gallery have continued to expand the collection over the years, so that you will see masterpieces from the Renaissance to Post-Impressionism. Most British and modern paintings are held at Tate Britain and Tate Modern respectively (see pages 21, 22).

Layout
There are four chronologically arranged sections. Early paintings by Duccio di Buoninsegna, Jan van Eyck, Piero della Francesca and others fill the Sainsbury Wing. The West Wing has 16th-century pictures, including Michelangelo's *Entombment*, while the North Wing is devoted to 17th-century artists such as Velázquez, Van Dyck, Rubens, Rembrandt and other painters of the Dutch school. Finally, the East Wing extends from the graceful 18th-century paintings of Chardin and Gainsborough, to the landscapes of Monet and Van Gogh, and the dawn of the 20th century, with Matisse and Picasso.

★ Highlights

The Ambassadors, Hans Holbein the Younger
Venus and Mars, Sandro Botticelli
Cartoon, Leonardo da Vinci
Pope Julius II, Raphael
Bacchus and Ariadne, Titian
The Arnolfini Portrait, Jan Van Eyck
Equestrian Portrait of Charles I, Van Dyck
The Triumph of Pan, Nicholas Poussin
Arabian Stallion, George Stubbs
The Hay Wain, John Constable

ℹ Information

⑩	Restaurant, cafe
⚹	Excellent
£	Free except for special exhibitions
+	Guided tours, lectures, films, picture option service

from Giotto to Cézanne

24

National Portrait Gallery

Walking through the National Portrait Gallery is a visual 'who's who' of British history, science and the arts. Even if not all the portraits are by great artists, they certainly portray the greatest men and women from Britain's past and present.

St Martin's Place WC2
T 020 7306 0055
Leicester Square or Charing Cross
Charing Cross
Daily 10–6 (Thurs and Fri 10–9)
npg.org.uk

Great Britons

Founded in 1856 to collect portraits of the most prominent figures in British society, the National Portrait Gallery spent its early years without a permanent home. Eventually, in 1896, it moved to its current building next to the National Gallery (see page 22), designed in the Florentine Renaissance style by Ewan Christie. There have been various extensions since then, including a special photography gallery in the 20th-century section. It is now the largest portrait collection in the world, containing oil paintings, watercolours, caricatures, silhouettes, photographs and busts.

★ Highlights

- *Henry VIII*, Hans Holbein the Younger
- *Samuel Pepys*, John Hayl
- *Queen Victoria*, Sir George Hayter
- *The Brontë Sisters*, Branwell Brontë
- *Isambard Kingdom Brunel*, John Callcot
- *Florence Nightingale*, William White
- *Self-portrait with Barbara Hepworth*, Ben Nicholson

Dead...

The galleries are arranged in chronological order, with the earliest on the top floor. Monarchs, inventors, merchants, engineers, explorers, empire builders, politicians and writers adorn the walls. The earliest dated portrait is of Henry VII (1505). You will find here the only known portrait of William Shakespeare. Other luminaries include Geoffrey Chaucer, Robert Clive of India, Winston Churchill and Margaret Thatcher.

...Or alive

Initially, the Victorians only allowed into the gallery portraits of those who were already dead, but this rule lapsed some time ago. Among contemporary portraits are those of footballer David Beckham with his wife Victoria, rock stars like Paul McCartney and David Bowie, and actors such as Joan Collins John Hurt and Stephen Fry. The gallery also sponsors the annual BP Portrait Award.

i Information

- Cafe, rooftop restaurant
- Good
- £ Free except for special exhibitions
- \+ Lectures, events

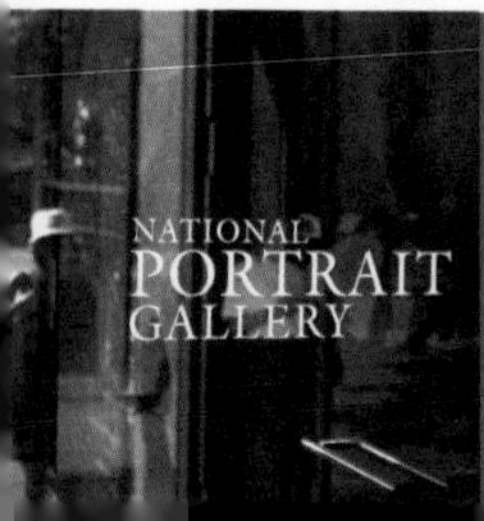

the largest portrait collection in the world

Natural History Museum

The Natural History Museum is the national museum of nature. It is made up of two sections: the Life Galleries follow the evolution of life on Earth, while the Earth Galleries concentrate on our planet itself.

🚇 **Cromwell Road SW7** (also entrance on Exhibition Road)

📞 020 7942 5000

⊖ South Kensington

🕸 Daily 10–5.50
nhm.ac.uk

Evolution

The Natural History Museum collection extends back to the mid-18th century when it formed part of the British Museum in Bloomsbury (see page 8). In 1881 it opened to the public in its own building in South Kensington, a splendid neo-Gothic pink and gold terracotta design by Alfred Waterhouse. In 1986, it incorporated the adjoining Geological Museum.

Life Galleries

The most popular exhibits tell the story of the dinosaurs. A plaster cast of the huge skeleton of a 150 million-year-old diplodocus (the original is in Pittsburgh, Pennsylvania) dominates the Central Hall, and if you turn left into Gallery 21 you will find more dinosaurs. Other exhibits include the human body, mammals, birds, the marine world and 'creepy crawlies', all illustrated by lots of slides, models and hands-on games.

Earth Galleries

The Earthquake Experience takes place in a Japanese supermarket, while the Restless Surface demonstrates the effects of natural forces on the Earth, and the Earth's Treasury focuses on the gemstones and minerals lying just beneath the Earth's crust. The Darwin Centre uses modern technology to make the most of the museum's collection of 70 million objects and the work of its 300 scientists accessible to people around the world.

★ Highlights
Cromwell Road façade
Giant gold nugget
Fossilised frogs
Afghan lapis lazuli
How the Memory Works
Restless Surface Gallery
Marine Invertebrate Gallery

i Information	
🍽	Restaurant, cafe, snack bar and picnic area
♿	Excellent
£	Free except for some special exhibitions
+	Regular tours, lectures, films, workshops

a collection of 70 million objects

Science Museum

If you want to find out how a plane flies, how Newton's reflecting telescope worked or how we receive satellite television, the Science Museum is the place to go. It answers these and many other questions in a highly accessible way, with plenty of hands-on displays.

Exhibition Road SW7
T 0870 870 4868
⊖ South Kensington

✹ Daily 10–6
sciencemuseum.org.uk

Science for all

Following on from the highly successful Great Exhibition of 1851, Prince Albert opened the South Kensington Museum in 1857, which incorporated what we now know as the Victoria and Albert Museum (see page 42) and the Science Museum. The latter moved into the current building in 1928.

The Wellcome Wing, which opened in 2000, increased the museum's size by 30%. Over six floors containing more than 60 collections, the narrative of man's industry and invention is related through various tools and products, from exquisite Georgian cabinets to a satellite launcher.

★ Highlights
Demonstrations
Taking part in Launch Pad
The hands-on basement area
Flight Lab
Apollo 10 module
Puffing Billy
Amy Johnson's aeroplane, *Jason*
18th-century watches and clocks
The Wellcome Wing
Historical characters explaining their achievements

Science is fun

Through entertaining displays, you can see how essential everyday objects such as the spinning wheel, steam engine, car and television were invented and developed. Plastic, for example, is vital for the functioning of our industrial society, but how do you make it? Or if you want to find out how to predict the weather or tides, or how to design a space rocket, here's your chance.

Science makes sense

You can use the hands-on equipment in Flight Lab to find out about the basic principles of flying; a motionride simulator of a Harrier Jump Jet cockpit makes you feel you are actually flying. The Wellcome Museum of the History of Medicine reveals the reality of prehistoric bone surgery, while the interactive Challenge of Materials explores the complexities of technology in an understandable way.

i Information
❢❍❢ Cafes, restaurant, picnic area
♿ Excellent; helpline 020 7942 4446
£ Free except for special exhibitions
+ Guided tours, demonstrations, historic characters, lectures, films, workshops

plenty of
hands-on
displays

30

Shakespeare's Globe

After many years of planning and fundraising, Shakespeare's Globe, a replica of the original 16th-century theatre where many of Shakespeare's plays were first performed, finally opened in 2000. This beautiful white circular building, with its thatched roof, recreates the exciting theatrical atmosphere of Shakespeare's time.

⌖ New Globe Walk, Bankside SE1
Theatre box office
T 020 7401 9919; matinee and evening performances during the summer. Exhibition and guided tour: 020 7902 1500

⊖ ⇌ London Bridge or Blackfriars
shakespeares-globe.org

Theatre
It was the American actor Sam Wanamaker who started the process of recreating Shakespeare's famous theatre, which burned down in 1613. The open-air theatre stages plays by Shakespeare and his contemporaries, sometimes with all-male casts (as in Shakespeare's time) and sometimes with all-female casts. You can stand in the uncovered area around the thrust stage as a 'groundling', and hope it does not rain, or sit on one of the sheltered wooden benches further back (in which case you may want to bring a cushion, or hire one there). Either way you will be sure to be caught up in the drama happening onstage in 'this wooden O'.

Exhibition and theatre tour
Beneath the theatre in the UnderGlobe, there is also a permanent, year-round exhibition about Shakespeare's London, Elizabethan theatre and the Bard's influence around the world. You can see how special effects were created in Shakespeare's time, watch a sword fighting display, add your voice to a scene played by Globe actors, and find out about Elizabethan clothing and musical instruments. After seeing the exhibition, you will be taken on a guided tour of the theatre itself.

★ Highlights
Seeing Shakespeare performed in the theatre
Exhibition and guided tour of theatre

ℹ Information
🍴 Restaurant, cafe
♿ Good
£ Moderate
+ Special events

Somerset House

Somerset House, on the north bank of the Thames, is one of the great Georgian buildings of London, with an elegant courtyard hosting concerts in the summer and ice-skating in the winter. It also contains three magnificent museums: the Courtauld Gallery, the Gilbert Collection and the Hermitage Rooms.

Strand WC2
Courtauld Gallery T 020 7848 2526
Gilbert Collection T 020 7420 9400
Hermitage Rooms T 020 7845 4600

⊖ ⇌ Charing Cross
✹ Daily 10–6
somerset-house.org.uk

Courtauld Gallery

The Courtauld Institute of Art Gallery has the finest collection of Impressionist and Post-Impressionist paintings in Britain, founded around the collection of Samuel Courtauld, the textile manufacturer. Other collections were added later, so there are also paintings, drawings, prints and sculptures by Old Masters such as Michelangelo, Rembrandt, Rubens and Goya.

Gilbert Collection

Donated by him to the nation in 1996, Sir Arthur Gilbert's magnificent collection of decorative arts, acquired over four decades, contains porcelain, furniture, clocks and miniatures. Displayed in 17 galleries, there are exceptional examples of European silver and gold work, as well as Roman enamel miniatures and Italian mosaics.

Hermitage Rooms

Decorated in the imperial style of the Winter Palace in the State Hermitage Museum in St Petersburg, the rooms house collections on loan from the Hermitage, one of the world's great museums with over three million artefacts. Unlike the Courtauld and Gilbert museums, the Hermitage Rooms do not have a permanent collection, so they are closed between exhibitions.

★ **Highlights**
Courtauld Gallery: Impressionists and Post-Impressionists
Gilbert Collection: silver and gold work
Hermitage Rooms: temporary exhibitions

i **Information**	
⊓⊖⊺	Cafes
⏦	Very good
£	Moderate (Courtauld Gallery free on Mon 10–2)
+	Talks, concerts, special exhibitions

St Paul's Cathedral

Listening to evensong amid the beautiful surroundings of St Paul's Cathedral is one of most tranquil and inspiring experiences in London. To avoid the crowds, it is best to go early or late.

🛈 **St Paul's Churchyard EC4**

T 020 7236 4128

⊖ St Paul's or Mansion House

⇌ City Thameslink, Blackfriars or Cannon Street

🕏 Mon–Sat 8.30–4.30 (last admission 4). Sung evensong Mon–Sat 5; Sun 3.15

stpauls.co.uk

Wren rebuilds London

Appointed the King's Surveyor-General in 1669, Christopher Wren was responsible for rebuilding the City, which had been decimated in the Great Fire of London. Twenty-three of the 51 churches he built are still standing, but his crowning glory is, of course, St Paul's Cathedral. Wren's epitaph on the floor beneath the dome reads: 'If you seek his monument, look around'.

The new St Paul's

Replacing the old St Paul's, which had been burnt down in the Fire, Wren's masterpiece is one of the few cathedrals ever to be designed by one architect and completed in his lifetime.

It was also the first in England to be built in the baroque style and to have a dome. The funerals of Admiral Lord Nelson, the Duke of Wellington and Sir Winston Churchill were held here. During World War II, when it survived the Blitz while buildings around it were bombed, St Paul's came to symbolise Britain's indomitable spirit.

Climbing to the galleries

There are three galleries in the dome. For the best views of the interior, climb the 259 steps to the Whispering Gallery, so-called because, due to its acoustics, something said on one side of the gallery can be heard on the opposite side. From here you will have fine views of Sir James Thornhill's frescoes on the dome above. Continue on to the exterior Stone Gallery, 378 steps from the bottom, then climb the remaining 172 steps to the Golden Gallery for more views of the city.

★ Highlights

Sung evensong
Frescoes and mosaics
Wren's Great Model in the Triforium
Triple-layered dome weighing 76,000 tons
Jean Tijou's sanctuary gates
Wellington's memorial
Light of the World, Holman Hunt
The Whispering Gallery
Wren's epitaph under the dome

𝒊 Information

🍽 Refectory in the crypt
♿ Very good
£ Expensive
+ Guided tours, organ recitals, masses in July

Tate Britain

Tate Britain houses the national collection of British art. Formerly, when the building was known as the Tate Gallery, it also contained the national modern art collection, but in 1999 this moved to the new building of Tate Modern (see page 38). This separation into two galleries gives visitors the opportunity to see more of the collection at any one time.

⊞ **Millbank SW1** (entrances on Millbank and Atterbury Street)

T 020 7887 8000

⊖ Pimlico

❋ Daily 10–5.50
(special exhibitions 10–5.40)
tate.org.uk

Henry Tate

The original Tate Gallery, designed by Sidney RJ Smith, opened in 1897, and was named after the sugar millionaire Henry Tate, who financed the building and donated his Victorian pictures to be displayed inside it. Various additions were made later, including the James Stirling's Clore Gallery in 1987, which houses the great Turner collection.

British art

Tate Britain covers five centuries of British art, from 1500 to the present day, incorporating paintings, drawings, photographs, sculptures and installations. You can move all the way from Tudor and Stuart portraits to contemporary conceptual art. Foreign artists who lived and worked in this country, such as Van Dyck and James Whistler, are represented.

The galleries are rehung periodically, and some paintings go into storage, but the most popular artists are always on display.

Best of British

Rooms are in rough chronological order, but are also themed, with 'Inventing Britain: Caricature', which features the 18th-century satirists Gillray, Rowlandson and Hogarth, and 'Art and Victorian Society', containing Pre-Raphaelites such as Dante Gabriel Rossetti and Edward Burne-Jones. Each year, the six shortlisted artists for the Turner Prize, Britain's most prestigious, if often controversial, art prize, are given a special exhibition here.

★ Highlights

Turner's watercolours

Flatford Mill, John Constable

Symphony in White No. 2, James Whistler

The Resurrection, Cookham, Stanley Spencer

Restaurant mural, Rex Whistler

The Turner Prize

_i_ Information

|❂| Restaurant, cafes

& Very good

£ Free except for special exhibitions

+ Talks, full education programme

the original
Tate Gallery

Tate Modern

Since 1999, Tate Modern has been the home of the national collection of modern art, which was formerly part of the Tate Gallery at Millbank. While the contents feature many international masterpieces, the transformed Bankside Power Station is also a major attraction in its own right.

🏛 **Bankside SE1**

T 020 7887 8888

⊖ Southwark or Blackfriars

⇌ London Bridge, Waterloo or Cannon Street

✴ Sun–Thurs 10-6;
Fri and Sat 10–10
tate.org.uk

Power to art

Sir Giles Gilbert Scott's gargantuan Bankside Power Station was converted by Swiss architects Herzog & de Meuron into a temple of modern art, while preserving the original building's essential features. The main change to the exterior was the addition of a glass structure on the roof to let in natural light. The awesome Turbine Hall is used for temporary exhibitions.

Modern art

In the permanent collection, the works are changed regularly, but always include items by the most influential artists of the 20th and 21st centuries, such as Matisse, Picasso, Epstein, Dalí, Pollock and Warhol. In paintings, drawings, sculptures, photographs and video, you can trace the history of modern art, from Cubism and Abstract Expressionism to Pop Art and Minimalism.

Collection

The collection is arranged by subject, for example: 'Nude/Action/Body', which contains works by Picasso and Spencer; 'History/Memory/Society', which includes Warhol's iconic *Marilyn Diptych*; and 'Landscape/Matter/Environment', with a whole room devoted to Rothko's Seagram Murals. Outside the gallery the landscape is pretty impressive too, with Norman Foster's Millennium Bridge stretching over to St Paul's Cathedral (see page 34) on the north side of the Thames.

⭐ **Highlights**

The Kiss, Auguste Rodin
The Grounds of the Château Noir, Paul Cézanne
The Three Dancers, Pablo Picasso
Seagram Murals, Mark Rothko
Marilyn Diptych, Andy Warhol
The Turbine Hall

ℹ **Information**

🍽 Restaurant, cafes

♿ Very good

£ Free except for special exhibitions

+ Lectures, tours, workshops and courses

The Tower has been a palace, fortress, state prison and execution site. There is plenty to see, including the Crown Jewels. Afterwards you might like to stroll round the corner to Tower Bridge, which has a fascinating museum.

ℹ Tower of London EC3

T 0870 756 6060

⊖ Tower Hill **⇄** Fenchurch Street, Cannon Street, London Bridge

✹ Mar–Oct: Tues–Sat 9–6; Sun–Mon 10–6. Nov–Feb: Tues–Sat 9–5; Sun–Mon 10–5 hrp.org.uk

ℹ Tower Bridge Exhibition SE1

T 020 7403 3761

⊖ Tower Hill

✹ Apr–Sept: 10–6.30 Oct–Mar: 9.30–6

towerbridge.org.uk

Norman fortress

William the Conqueror began building the Tower of London soon after the conquest in 1066. The oldest surviving parts are the White Tower, which now houses a display of armour, and the Chapel of St John. Beside Traitor's Gate, the notorious river entrance to the Tower, is the Medieval Palace, built by Edward I.

Imprisonment and execution

It was from the Bloody Tower that the 'Princes in the Tower', the sons of the late Edward IV, vanished in 1483 while in the care of their uncle, who was then crowned Richard III. The Tower is perhaps most famous as the site of the execution of Henry VIII's wives Anne Boleyn and Catherine Howard, which took place on Tower Green.

The Crown Jewels

The Crown Jewels include the Imperial State Crown, which contains the Second Star of Africa diamond, and the Queen Consort's Crown, with the famous Koh-i-Noor diamond. The 'Crowns and Diamonds' exhibition in the Martin Tower is very informative.

Tower Bridge

Tower Bridge opened in 1894, and is the most distinctive and distinguished of London's landmarks. Step inside the Tower Bridge Exhibition and enjoy stunning views of London from 45 metres (147 feet) above the Thames, learn about how and why Tower Bridge was built, and visit the Victorian Engine Rooms, where the original steam engines still remain today. The bridge lifts up about 900 times a year to let tall vessels pass beneath it.

★ Highlights

Tower of London: Medieval Palace; Raleigh's room; Imperial State Crown; Tower ravens; Grand Punch Bowl, 1829; St John's Chapel

Tower Bridge Exhibition: views from high-level walkways; Victorian Engine Rooms

ℹ Information

🍽 Tower of London: cafes, restaurant

♿ Tower: excellent for Jewel House

£ Tower: very expensive

£ Tower Bridge: moderate

+ Tower: free tours every 30 minutes by Yeoman Warders

+ Tower Bridge: special events

Crowns and Diamonds

Victoria and Albert Museum

The variety and richness of the V&A collection of arts and crafts is breathtaking. You never know what each room will reveal: a French boudoir, plaster casts of classical sculptures or exquisite contemporary glass. What is certain is that you will make some amazing discoveries.

Cromwell Road SW7 (another entrance on Exhibition Road)

T 020 7942 2000

⊖ South Kensington

♿ Daily 10–5.45; Wed and last Fri of month 10–10

vam.ac.uk

Enlightenment

The brainchild of the enlightened Prince Albert, the V&A started as the South Kensington Museum in 1857. Housed in Aston Webb's splendid 1890 building, the V&A has expanded enormously over the years, so that it is now the world's largest decorative arts museum (and contains the national sculpture collection).

Bigger and better

The V&A is far too big to cover in one day, with four million objects in 145 galleries on six floors. So the best way to proceed is either to take one of the guided tours or to study the floor plan and select the rooms whose contents appeal to you the most. That may include the Dress Collection, featuring clothes from modern-day designers such as Versace and Issey Miyake; the Morris, Gamble and Poynter rooms, decorated in the styles of these three leading designers and artists; or the Nehru Gallery of Indian Art, with the ever-popular Tipu's Tiger.

Ancient and modern

Larger museum objects include whole London house façades, grand rooms and the Raphael Cartoons. The Cast Rooms contain life-sized reproductions and casts of famous statues, including Michelangelo's David and parts of Trajan's Column from Rome. However, not everything here is old; the museum has always been keen to buy contemporary work. For example, more than 60% of furniture entering the building is 20th century, as the V&A continues to update and improve its collection.

★ Highlights
Medieval ivory carvings
Jones porcelain collection
Glass Gallery
Shah Jahan's Jade Cup
Canning Jewel
New Raphael Gallery
Frank Lloyd Wright Room
British Galleries
The Hereford Screen
The Great Bed of Ware
Tipu's Tiger

_i_ Information	
🍴	Basement restaurant, cafe
♿	Very good
£	Free (except for special exhibitions)
+	Guided tours, lectures, courses, concerts

clothes from modern-day designers

4 million objects in 145 galleries

Westminster Abbey

In addition to being a place of worship, Westminster Abbey has been the setting for the coronations and funerals of many monarchs, and the final resting place for some of the most famous people from the last one thousand years of British history.

🚇 **Broad Sanctuary SW1**
(entry by North Door)

T 020 7654 4900
Services
T 020 7222 5152

⊖ Westminster or St James's Park
⇌ Victoria
westminster-abbey.org

Royal abbey

It was Edward the Confessor who began the rebuilding of the modest Benedictine abbey church of St Peter, which was consecrated in 1065. The abbey has always been closely connected to royalty: from William I, all sovereigns have been crowned here, and up to George II, all were buried here.

History of the abbey

Of the original abbey, only the Pyx Chamber and the Norman undercroft remain. The gothic nave and choir were rebuilt by Henry III in the 13th century – the Chapter House, dating from 1253, still has its original floor tiles. The Henry VIII Chapel (which contains the tombs of Elizabeth I and her half-sister Mary I, and inside the main chapel, the tomb of Henry VII himself) was added in the early 16th century. Finally, the West Towers (by Nicholas Hawksmoor) date from 1745.

Monuments and memorials

All around, you will see monuments to statesmen. Poets' Corner is in the south transept, where many of the nation's most distinguished poets are buried or commemorated. Around the 19th-century choir screen is Scientists' Corner, with memorials to Sir Isaac Newton and others. Finally, near the West Door exit is the Tomb of the Unknown Warrior.

★ Highlights
Portrait of Richard II
Sir Isaac Newton memorial
Sir James Thornhill's window
Edward the Confessor's Chapel
Tile floor, Chapter House
Weekday sung evensong (except Wed) at 5pm

i Information	
🍴	Cafe in cloisters
♿	Good
£	Services free. Royal chapels moderate
+	Guided tours

setting for coronations and funerals

🔷 Museums and galleries

Apsley House

Residence of the Duke of Wellington. Magnificent paintings, porcelain, silver, furniture, sculpture and memorabilia.

Hyde Park Corner W1

english-heritage.org.uk/apsleyhouse

T 020 7499 5676

✺ Tues–Sun, Apr–Oct 10–5; Nov–Mar 10–4

⊖ Hyde Park Corner

Banqueting House

Built by Inigo Jones in 1619–22 for James I; where Charles I was beheaded in 1649. The only important part of Whitehall Palace to escape the fire of 1698.

Whitehall SW1

hrp.org.uk/webcode/banquet_home.asp

T 0870 751 5178

✺ Mon–Sat 10–5

⊖ Charing Cross, Embankment or Westminster.

≈ Charing Cross

Cabinet War Rooms

The underground headquarters for Winston Churchill's War Cabinet during World War II.

Clive Steps, King Charles St SW1

cwr.iwm.org.uk

T 020 7930 6961

✺ Daily 9.30–6

⊖ St James's Park or Westminster

Dalí Universe

Over 500 of Salvador Dalí's paintings, sculptures and furniture.

County Hall Gallery,
Riverside Building,
Westminster Bridge Road SE1

countyhallgallery.com

T 0870 744 7485

✺ Daily 10–6.30

⊖ ≈ Waterloo

Design Museum

Founded by design guru Terence Conran to stimulate design awareness. Good shop.

Butler's Wharf, Shad Thames SE1

designmuseum.org

T 0870 833 9955

✺ Daily 10–5.45

⊖ Tower Hill or London Bridge.

≈ London Bridge, Tower Gateway

Dickens House

The world-famous novelist worked on *Pickwick Papers, Oliver Twist, Nicholas Nickleby* and *Barnaby Rudge* during his three years here.

48 Doughty Street WC1

dickensmuseum.com

T 020 7405 2127

✺ Mon–Sat 10–5; Sun 11–5

⊖ Russell Square, Chancery Lane, Holborn

Dr Johnson's House

Dr Samuel Johnson lived here from 1748 to 1759, and compiled the first definitive English dictionary.

17 Gough Square EC4

drjohnsonshouse.org

T 020 7353 3745

✺ May–Sept: Mon–Sat 11–5.30; Oct–Apr: Mon–Sat 11–5

⊖ ≈ Blackfriars, Temple, Holborn, Chancery Lane

Dulwich Picture Gallery

European art, mostly from the 17th century. This was the first purpose-built art gallery in England.

Gallery Road SE21

dulwichpicturegallery.org.uk

T 020 8693 5254

✺ Tues–Fri 10–5; Sat, Sun, Bank Hols 11–5

≈ West Dulwich, North Dulwich

Charles Dickens' writing desk

Cabinet War Rooms

SAMUEL JOHNSON
BORN AT LICHFIELD, Sept 18th 1709

Other major attractions

Hayward Gallery
Part of the South Bank Arts Centre, featuring current international art shows.

South Bank Centre SE1

hayward.org.uk

T 020 7921 0813

Mon, Thurs, Sat, Sun 10–6; Tues, Wed 10–8; Fri 10–9.
Closed between exhibitions

⊖ ⇌ Waterloo

Institute of Contemporary Arts
ICA is a centre for international contemporary arts, with three galleries, two cinemas and a theatre.

Nash House, The Mall SW1

ica.org.uk

T 020 7930 3647/0493

Daily (call for details)

⊖ Piccadilly Circus or Charing Cross

National Army Museum
The story of the British soldier from Tudor times to the present day.

Royal Hospital Road SW3

national-army-museum.ac.uk

T 020 7730 0717

Daily 10–5.30

⊖ Sloane Square

Royal Academy of Arts
Major art shows, plus the annual Summer Exhibition.

Burlington House, Piccadilly W1

royalacademy.org.uk

T 020 7300 8000

Sat–Thurs 10–6; Fri 10–10

⊖ Green Park or Piccadilly

Royal Hospital Chelsea
Founded in 1682 by King Charles II for veteran soldiers – the famous Chelsea Pensioners in their scarlet coats.

chelsea-pensioners.co.uk

Royal Hospital Road SW3

T 020 7881 5200

Daily 10–12 and 2–4; Chapel open to public for services on Sun; Museum closed Sun (Mar–Oct only)

⊖ Sloane Square

Saatchi Gallery
Home to advertising mogul Charles Saatchi's famous contemporary art collection. Due to re-open in 2007, the gallery will be situated in the Duke of York's HQ, Chelsea, and will cover a massive 50,000 sq ft. See saatchi-gallery.co.uk for more on this.

Sir John Soane's Museum
This classical architect left his house, collection and library to the nation on his death in 1837.

13 Lincoln's Inn Fields WC2

soane.org

T 020 7405 2107

Tues–Sat 10–5 (late evening opening on first Tues of each month 6–9)

⊖ Holborn

Theatre Museum

Lively museum in Covent Garden, which contains the national collections of the performing arts.

Russell Street WC2

theatremuseum.org

- **T** 020 7943 4700
- Tues–Sun 10–6
- Covent Garden, Charing Cross or Leicester Square

Wallace Collection

Paintings, armour, ceramics and furniture in an 18th-century townhouse.

Hertford House, Manchester Square W1

wallacecollection.org

- **T** 020 7563 9500
- Daily 10–5
- Bond Street, Baker Street

Whitechapel Art Gallery

Specialises in modern and contemporary art.

80–82 Whitechapel High Street E1

whitechapel.org

- **T** 020 7522 7888
- Tues–Sun 11–6; Thurs 11–9
- Aldgate East

✪ Cathedrals and churches

Holy Trinity, Sloane Street

Late-Gothic Revival church with Arts and Crafts interior by Morris, and glass by Burne-Jones.

Sloane Street SW7

- **T** 020 7730 7270
- Mon–Fri 8–5.45; Sat 9–4.45; Sun 8.30–1
- Sloane Square

Oratory of St Philip Neri

Also known as the Brompton or London Oratory (1876). Fine baroque interior.

Brompton Road SW7

bromptonoratory.com

- **T** 020 7808 0900
- Daily 6.30am–8pm
- South Kensington

St Clement Danes Church

The interior was destroyed during World War II, but restored in the 1950s. Central church of the Royal Air Force, with the bells of the famous 'Oranges and Lemons' nursery rhyme.

Strand WC2

rafcom.co.uk/information/church.cfm

- **T** 020 7242 8282
- Daily 9–4.30
- Embankment or Temple

St James's, Piccadilly

Built in the 1680s for the local aristocracy, this Wren church has a sumptuous interior.

197 Piccadilly SW1

st-james-piccadilly.org

- **T** 020 7734 4511
- Daily 8.30–6.30
- Piccadilly Circus or Green Park

St Martin-in-the-Fields

Concerts at lunchtime Mon, Tues and Fri, and in evening Thurs, Fri and Sat (020 7839 8362).

Trafalgar Square WC2

stmartin-in-the-fields.org

- **T** 020 7766 1100
- Mon–Sat 10–8; Sun 12–8

St Mary-le-Bow Church

A Wren church defining the true Cockney, who must be born within the sound of its famous Bow Bells.

Cheapside EC2

stmarylebow.co.uk

- **T** 020 7248 5139
- Mon–Thurs 6.30–6; Fri 6.30–4
- St Paul's, Bank or Mansion House

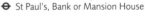

Southwark Cathedral
Atmospheric of its medieval origins, despite much rebuilding; fine choir and monuments.
Montague Close SE1
southwark.anglican.org/cathedral/
T 020 7367 6700
✹ Mon–Fri 8–6; Sun 9–7
⊖ ⇌ London Bridge

Westminster Cathedral
Largest and most important Roman Catholic church in England, with Byzantine-style architecture. Fine marbles and mosaics and 87.5-metre (284-foot) tower.
Victoria Street SW1
westminstercathedral.org.uk
T 020 7798 9055
✹ Sun–Fri 7–7; Sat 8–7. Tower Mar–Nov, daily 9.30–12.30 and 1–5; Dec–Feb, Thurs–Sun 9.30–12.30 and 1–5
⊖ ⇌ Victoria, St James's Park

⭐ Statues and monuments

Burghers of Calais
Auguste Rodin's muscular bronze citizens (1915).
Victoria Tower Gardens SW1
⊖ Westminster

Charles I
This superb equestrian statue was made by Hubert Le Sueur in 1633.
South side of Trafalgar Square
⊖ ⇌ Charing Cross

Cleopatra's Needle
The 26-metre (85-foot) pink-granite obelisk made in 1450 BC records the triumphs of Ramses the Great.
Victoria Embankment WC2

⊖ Embankment

Eros
Alfred Gilbert's memorial (1893) to the philanthropic 7th Earl of Shaftesbury actually portrays the Angel of Christian Charity, not Eros.
Piccadilly Circus W1
⊖ Piccadilly Circus

Monument
Wren's 61.5-metre (202-foot) Doric column commemorates the Great Fire of London (1666). Worth climbing the dark corkscrew of 311 steps for the glorious view.
Monument Street EC3
T 020 7626 2717
✹ Daily 10–6
⊖ Monument

Nelson's Column
Horatio, Viscount Nelson (1758–1805) went up onto his 52-metre (171-foot) column in 1843.
Trafalgar Square WC2
⊖ ⇌ Charing Cross

Oliver Cromwell
Cromwell, Lord Protector of England from 1653 to 1658, looks across Parliament Square.
Houses of Parliament SW1
⊖ Westminster

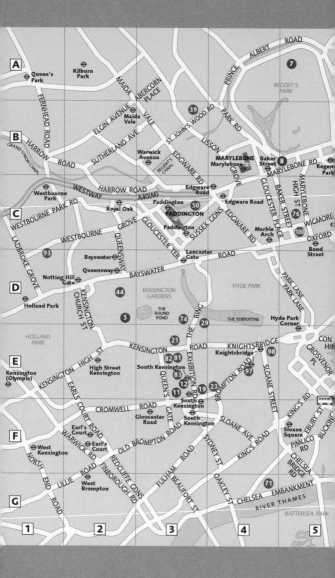

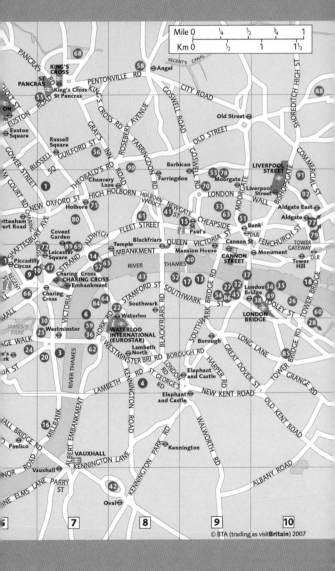

© BTA (trading as visit**Britain**) 2007

see overleaf for key

Key

▬▬▬	Motorway
▬▬▬	Main road
▬▬▬	Minor road
▬▬▬	Shopping street
▬▬▬	Jubilee walkway
▬▬▬	Canal, dock, lake, river
●	Launch
⊖	DLR
▬▬▬	Railway
⇌	Station
⊖	Underground
EXPRESS LINK TO STANSTED	Rail Express Link to Airport
SHUTTLE BUS TO CITY AIRPORT	Links to City Airport
▬▬▬	Building
⬤	Changing the guard
●	Top 20 attractions
⬛	Market
▬▬▬	Park
✡✝☾	Places of worship
i	Tourist Information Centre
▲	Youth hostel

Top twenty

1 British Museum — C7
2 Buckingham Palace — E6
3 Houses of Parliament and Big Ben — E7
4 Imperial War Museum — E8
5 Kensington Palace — D2
6 British Airways London Eye — D7
7 London Zoo — A5
8 Madame Tussauds — B5
9 National Gallery — D6
10 National Portrait Gallery — D7
11 Natural History Museum — E3
12 Science Museum — E3
13 Shakespeare's Globe — D9
14 Somerset House — D7
15 St Paul's Cathedral — C9
16 Tate Britain — F7
17 Tate Modern — D9
18 Tower of London and Tower Bridge Exhibition — D10
19 Victoria and Albert Museum — E3
20 Westminster Abbey — E7
21 Albert Memorial — E3
22 BFI London Imax Cinema — D8

Other attractions

23 Brompton Oratory — E4
24 Central Hall Westminster — E6
25 Churchill Museum and Cabinet War Rooms — E6
26 City Hall — D10
27 Clink Prison — D9
28 *Cutty Sark* — E10
29 Diana Memorial Fountain — D3
30 Downing Street — E7
31 Eros — D6
32 Golden Hinde — D9
33 Guildhall — C9
34 Hay's Galleria — D10
35 HMS *Belfast* — D10

36 London Aquarium	E7
37 London Bridge	D9
38 The London Dungeon	D10
39 Lord's Cricket Ground	B3
40 Millennium Bridge	D9
41 Old Bailey	C8
42 Oval Cricket Ground	G8
43 Oxo Tower	D8
44 Diana Memorial Playground	D2
45 Southwark Cathedral	D9
46 Spencer House	D6
47 St Martin-in-the-Fields	D7
48 Westminster Cathedral	E6
49 Winston Churchill's Britain at War Exhibition	D10
50 Alexander Fleming Museum	C3

Museums & galleries

51 Bank of England Museum	C9
52 Bankside Gallery	D8
53 Barbican Art Gallery	C9
54 Bramah Tea and Coffee Museum	D9
55 British Library	B7
56 Charles Dickens Museum	B7
57 Courtauld Gallery	D7
58 Crafts Council Gallery	A8
59 Dalí Universe	E7
60 Design Museum	D10
61 Dr Johnson's House	C8
62 Florence Nightingale Museum	E7
63 Guildhall Art Gallery	C9
64 Hayward Gallery	D7
65 Hermitage Rooms	D7
66 ICA Gallery	D6
67 Jewish Museum	A5
68 London Canal Museum	A7
69 London's Transport Museum	D7

70 Museum of London	C9
71 National Army Museum	G4
72 Photographers' Gallery	D7
73 Royal Academy of Arts	D6
74 Serpentine Gallery	D3
75 Sir John Soane's Museum	C7
76 Wallace Collection	C5
77 Whitechapel Art Gallery	C10

Halls & exhibition venues

78 Barbican Centre	C9
79 ExCel	C10
80 New Connaught Rooms	C7
81 Royal Albert Hall	E3
82 Royal College of Art	E3
83 Royal College of Music	E3
84 South Bank Centre	D7

Markets

85 Bermondsey	E10
86 Borough Market	D9
87 Camden Lock	A6
88 Columbia Road	A10
89 Covent Garden	D7
90 Leather Lane	B8
91 Old Spitalfields	C10
92 Petticoat Lane	C10
93 Portobello Road	D1

Famous-name stores

94 Burberry	D5
95 Fortnum & Mason	D6
96 Hamleys	C6
97 Harrods	E4
98 Harvey Nichols	E4
99 Liberty	C6
100 Selfridges	C5

Parks and gardens

Hyde Park

One of London's largest open spaces, Hyde Park became the first royal park to be opened to the public in 1637.

- **⚏** W2
- **T** 020 7298 2100
- **⊖** Marble Arch, Lancaster Gate, Queensway, Knightsbridge or Hyde Park
- **✿** Daily 5am–midnight
- **⦿** Restaurant, cafe
- **+** Pop concerts and military bands in summer

  royalparks.gov.uk

It was the setting for the hugely influential Great Exhibition of 1851.

The north-east corner used to be called Tyburn, a gallows where public executions took place regularly. Today it is known as Speakers' Corner, where (especially on Sunday afternoons) soapbox orators – and hecklers – gather to debate current topics.

Nearby is Marble Arch, designed by John Nash in 1828 and based on the triumphal arch of Constantine in Rome – it was originally the grand gateway to Buckingham Palace, but was moved here in 1851 when Victoria and Albert needed more room to extend the palace.

In the south-west of the park you can visit the Princess Diana Memorial Fountain, a great ring of white Cornish granite in which water swirls and twists.

Other activities include swimming in the Serpentine and horse riding on Rotten Row. Although the park is open until late, it is best to avoid it after dark.

58

Parks and gardens

Kew Gardens

Named as a World Heritage Site by UNESCO in 2003, the Royal Botanic Gardens, Kew contains 44,000 different plants and glorious greenhouses scattered over 120 hectares (300 acres).

🏠 **Kew Road, Kew**
T 020 8332 5655
⊖ Kew Gardens
⇌ Kew Bridge

🌼 Daily from 9.30am; closing hrs vary
🍽 Restaurants, cafes
+ Guided tours 11 and 2 from Victoria Gate; orchid show Feb–Mar
rbgkew.org.uk

The gardens were started around Kew Palace in 1759. Architect Sir William Chambers built the Pagoda, Orangery, Ruined Arch and three temples.

Later George III enlarged the gardens to their present size and Sir Joseph Banks (head gardener 1772–1819), who had travelled with Captain Cook, planted them with specimens from all over the world.

The gardens were given to the nation in 1841, and many other additions have been made since then. There are wonderful greenhouses, such as the Palm House, the Temperate House and the stunning new Alpine House, as well as lovely walks in woods and by lakes. Of note is the new John Pawson-designed bridge – the Sackler Crossing – which crosses the lake in the western end of the park. The Evolution House displays an interactive exhibition, which tells the story of plants through the centuries.

As the seasons change, Kew offers a variety of activities. In high season Kew Palace (operated by Historic Royal Palaces) and the pagoda are open to visitors; at Easter there is a petting zoo for children; and over Christmas an ice rink is installed, so transforming the Kew landscape.

Kew's unmatched contribution over the years to plant conservation is reflected in its motto: 'All life depends on plants'.

Parks and gardens

The Regent's Park

The Regent's Park is one of London's most popular retreats from the bustle of the city.

- Marylebone Road NW1
- T 020 7486 7905
  Theatre bookings
- T 0870 0601 811 (May–Sept only)
- Baker Street, Regent's Park, Great Portland Street or Camden Town

- Daily 5am–dusk
- Restaurants, cafes
- + Boats for hire; and summer weekend bandstand music; open-air theatre
  royalparks.gov.uk

It was conceived as part of a grand design of Prince Regent (later George IV) and his architect, John Nash, to bring elegance to London's landscape, The Regent's Park now has stunning rose gardens with more than 30,000 roses of 400 varieties.

Originally intended to be used as pleasure gardens by the aristocracy, the park has been open to the public since 1835, when the adjoining Regent's Canal was one of the busiest waterways in Britain. It is now popular for boat trips and bankside walks.

The park is the largest outdoor sports area in London, with a spectacular community sports pavilion, known as the Hub, as well as sports pitches, covering almost 40 hectares (100 acres).

It is also home to London Zoo (see page 18), a boating lake, a Wildfowl Breeding Centre, Queen Mary's Garden and an open-air theatre staging summer performances and lunchtime and evening concerts in the bandstands.

There are several cafes in the park, one of which – The Garden Cafe – was voted *Time Out*'s top park cafe in 2005.

Parks and gardens

Kensington Gardens

Having moved into Kensington Palace (see page 16) in the early 18th century, Queen Anne annexed a part of the royal Hyde Park to form Kensington Gardens.

- ▣ W8
- T 020 7298 2217
- ⊖ Bayswater, Lancaster Gate, High Street Kensington or Queensway

- ❋ Daily 6am to dusk
- ⦿ Cafe in the Orangery
- + Puppet shows in summer
  royalparks.gov.uk/parks/
  kensington_gardens

George II's wife, Queen Caroline, followed on by creating the Round Pond and Long Water to complete the 111-hectare (275-acre) gardens.

These royal gardens may merge into Hyde Park, but they still possess a distinct, formal identity. The awesome 55-metre-high (180-foot) Albert Memorial, opposite the Royal Albert Hall, is one of the great Victorian sculptures. It was designed by Sir George Gilbert Scott in 1872–76 and features a statue of Prince Albert in a neo-Gothic shrine, as well as a frieze containing 169 carved figures.

Also worth seeing is Peter Pan, George Frampton's 1912 statue of JM Barrie's fairy-tale creation, the boy who never grew up.

The park has a boating lake, and contemporary art exhibitions are on show at the Serpentine Gallery.

The Diana, Princess of Wales' Memorial Playground – opened in June 2000, in memory of the late Princess – is a children's wonderland. Its centrepiece is a huge, wooden pirate ship.

Parks and gardens

London Wetland Centre

The award-winning London Wetland Centre is the first project of its kind in the world – more than 40 hectares (99 acres) of man-made wetlands within the bounds of a great city.

- W13
- **T** 020 8409 4400
- Hammersmith, then 'Duck Bus' no. 283 from stand C
- Daily 9.30–6 in summer; 9.30–5 in winter
- Cafe, restaurant
- + Wetlands exhibition, art gallery, children's discovery centre
  wwt.org.uk/visit/wetlandcentre

The shallow lakes and waterways that fringe Barnes are one of London's great surprise packages – an expanse of protected wetlands within city bounds. Run by the Wildfowl and Wetlands Trust, the London Wetland Centre was designated a Site of Special Scientific Interest (SSSI) within two years of its grand opening in 2000.

To many people, these tranquil wetlands serve simply as an oasis – a welcome breather from city life. It's not just bird-lovers who are drawn here; the centre is popular with children and local artists, who come to capture the beauty of these meandering waterways, which are alive year-round with birds, bats, amphibians, water voles and dragonflies.

Threaded by boardwalks, a mosaic of lakes, ponds and lagoons is divided into 14 different wetland habitats, from an Australian billabong to Siberian tundra.

Viewing the wildlife couldn't be easier, with a series of hides, the three-storey Peacock Tower and glass observatory, complete with art gallery and restaurant. The visitor centre even has CCTV links to the hides, enabling visitors to glimpse the action in comfort. Regular courses and events are staged at the London Wetland Centre, including the popular 'Introduction to Birdwatching' course.

Among the 140 species of birds to be observed are a whole range of rare wetland birds, many of which are breeding successfully at the centre. Lapwing, redshank, snipe, pochard, reed and sedge warbler can all be seen, as well as birds of prey, such as peregrine falcons and marsh harriers. The centre also supports nationally important numbers of Gadwall and Shoveler duck. If you visit towards dusk, listen out for the warble of the marsh frogs.

Docklands

St Katharine Docks, near Tower Hill, marks the start of London's Docklands, which stretch eastward along the north bank of the Thames past Canary Wharf.

Distance: Walk approximately 1.5 miles (3km)

Time: 3–4 hours (walk and DLR), including stops

Start Point: St Katharine Docks, Tower Hill

End Point: Island Gardens

Lunch: Prospect of Whitby, 57 Wapping Wall

T 020 7481 1095

Significant commercial activity in the docks stopped decades ago, but the rejuvenation of the Docklands began in 1981, and the site now has new homes, offices and a number of visitor attractions. It's best to do the walk on a weekday when the area is much more lively. After having a look round the former dockyard of St Katharine Docks, follow St Katharine's Way along the river to Wapping High Street. The old warehouses along here have now been converted into luxury apartments. At Wapping Pier Head there are some elegant Georgian houses, which used to belong to rich wharf owners. Beyond Waterside Gardens you can see the baroque church of St George-in-the-East.

If it is pub-opening time (after 11.30am or noon on Sunday) carry on to the old Prospect of Whitby pub, once the haunt of artists painting the river. From there, retrace your steps a short way along Wapping Wall, turn right into Garnet Street, cross the main street known as the Highway, and then immediately turn left into Dellow Street, which leads to Shadwell Docklands Light Railway (DLR) station. Take the train to Island Gardens.

the
rejuvenation
of Docklands

The overland journey has great views from the raised track over the impressive post-modernist developments in the centre of the Docklands – a sort of glimpse into the future. Explore the Museum in Docklands, in a former Georgian warehouse. This explains the story of London's river, port and people, from Roman times to the present day. Nearby is Canary Wharf, which includes the 267-metre (875-foot) Canary Wharf Tower (Britain's tallest building) and places to eat, drink and shop.

End your journey at Island Gardens, where there are superb views south across the river to Greenwich. Reboard the train and return to central London on the DLR back to Tower Gateway (or as far as Canary Wharf, then take the Jubilee Underground line west), or take a boat from Greenwich Pier to Westminster Pier (see Families and kids, River trips, pages 74–78).

★ Highlights

St Katherine's Dock
Church of St-George-in-the East
Docklands Light Railway
Museum in Docklands
Canary Wharf
Island Gardens

Britain's tallest building

Greenwich

This walk is a journey through Greenwich's maritime, astronomical and royal history. It is best to do it at the weekend, which is when the markets are open.

Distance: Walk approximately 2 miles (3.2km)

Time: 2 hours, but allow additional time for visits

Start Point: Greenwich Pier

Travel by boat from Westminster Pier – allow an hour for the boat journey

End Point: Greenwich Pier

Lunch: Trafalgar Tavern, Park Row

T 020 8858 2437

Ahead you can see the tall-masted ship *Cutty Sark*. Launched in 1869, it was the fastest tea-clipper of its day. The small yacht nearby is the *Gypsy Moth IV*, in which Sir Francis Chichester made the first solo voyage around the world in 1966–7. From here, walk back past Greenwich Pier and east along the river. The Old Royal Naval Hospital (until recently a Royal Naval School, but now part of the University of Greenwich) is on the right, built on the site of Greenwich Palace. The hall and chapel are open to the public.

Continue along the river path to the Trafalgar Tavern in Park Row for a lunch break. The entrance to the Queen's House and National Maritime Museum is ahead on the right. The museum is packed with naval instruments, charts, models, paintings and nautical memorabilia. Exit back into Park Row and enter Greenwich Park.

Follow the first path in front of the Queen's House until you can turn right, then take the second path to the left which climbs steeply up One Tree Hill. From here make your way towards the Old Royal Observatory, the red-brick building with the green dome on the next hill, built by Sir Christopher Wren for King Charles II. It has exhibits on the history of astronomy and time. You can straddle the Prime Meridian at 0 degrees longitude.

With your back to the statue of General Wolfe (who captured Quebec in 1759), walk along Blackheath Road. At the small roundabout turn right onto a path that follows a line of trees to a gate in the park wall. Turn left along the gravel drive to Croom's Hill. Towards the bottom of the hill you will find the only Fan Museum in the world.

Continue to the bottom of Croom's Hill, then walk ahead into Stockwell Street – the village market is on the right – and turn right into Greenwich Church Street. The entrance to the craft market is through an alleyway to the right. Return to Greenwich Church Street, turn right, cross College Approach, and after 91 metres (100 yards) you'll be back at the *Cutty Sark*.

To return to central London, either get on another boat or board the Docklands Light Railway (DLR) at the nearby *Cutty Sark* for Maritime Greenwich station.

★ Highlights
Cutty Sark
Royal Naval Hospital (Painted Hall & Chapel)
Queen's House
National Maritime Museum
Greenwich Park
Old Royal Observatory & Prime Meridian

Millennium Bridge

A stroll across the Thames from St Paul's Cathedral to Tate Modern, then on to Shakespeare's Globe, the *Golden Hinde*, Southwark Cathedral and Borough Market.

Distance: Walk approximately 2 miles (3.2km) on foot

Time: 3–5 hours including stops

Start point: St Paul's Cathedral

End Point: George Inn, Borough High Street

Lunch: Anchor Pub, 34 Park Street, **T** 020 7407 1577

The Millennium Bridge is the first new bridge to appear in central London in over a century. It connects the two great landmarks of St Paul's Cathedral and Tate Modern, the old and the new, and links the City with the multiple attractions of the South Bank. The winning design for the bridge was chosen by the Royal Institute of British Architects from more than 200 proposals. The structure is a shallow suspension bridge, four-metres (13 feet) wide, with cables that run alongside the deck, rather than above, allowing for unimpeded views of the London skyline.

Begin your walk at St Paul's Cathedral, Sir Christopher Wren's mighty landmark overlooking the Square Mile – site of London's earliest settlements. The cathedral serves as a final resting place for national heroes, and as a site for jubilee celebrations and royal weddings (page 34).

Head south from St Paul's, past the Blitz Memorial and on to the Millennium Bridge, enjoying the views upriver towards Tower Bridge

and downriver towards the London Eye. At the end of the bridge stands Tate Modern (see page 38), set in the old Bankside Power Station, an imposing structure comprising four million bricks and a 95.5-metre (325-foot) chimney. Tate Modern is Britain's national gallery of international modern art.

Next to Tate Modern, to the east, stands the remarkable Shakespeare's Globe (see page 30), an exact replica of the original, thatched theatre in which Shakespeare himself performed. The Globe's towering oak frame is secured with more than 6,000 wooden pegs; its plastered walls are whitewashed with a mixture of sand, slaked lime and animal hair; and its galleries are roofed with Norfolk thatch.

From the Globe, head briefly east along Bankside then turn south into Bear Gardens, which was the site of the Hope Theatre in the mid-17th century. Bear baiting was hugely popular at this time, and the theatre doubled up as a bear-baiting arena. At the end of Bear Gardens, turn left onto Park Street past the site of the

Rose Theatre, a competitor to the Globe during Shakespeare's time. At the end of Park Street, head left towards the river and you come to the Anchor Pub, a good place for a historic drink, and a bite to eat. Samuel Pepys witnessed the Great Fire of London from this very pub back in 1666. From beer to wine, if you stop by Vinopolis just round the corner. Set beneath the arches of a Victorian railway viaduct, this museum is dedicated entirely to the history and pleasures of wine.

Next, head along Clink Street, site of the notorious Clink Prison (hence the phrase 'in the clink'), established in 1171 and burnt down during the Gordon Riots of 1780. Just off Clink Street, berthed at St Mary Overie Dock, is the *Golden Hinde*, a full-sized reconstruction of the 16th-century warship in which Sir Francis Drake circumnavigated the globe.

From the *Golden Hinde*, it's just a short hop to Southwark Cathedral, built on the site of a pagan shrine, then a Roman Villa. The cathedral is an interesting medley of architecture, thanks to more than a thousand years of restoration and reconstruction. Right next to Southwark Cathedral is Borough Market, first recorded in 1014. The market reached its height in Victorian times, when it became known as 'London's Larder' – and has experienced a great resurgence in recent years.

Finish your walk at the timber-framed George Inn, just off Borough High Street. First recorded in 1542, the George is London's only remaining coaching inn, with two tiers of galleries set around an attractive quadrangle.

★ Highlights
St Paul's
Millennium Bridge
Tate Modern
Shakespeare's Globe
Golden Hinde
Southwark Cathedral
Borough Market

BFI London IMAX Cinema

Biggest screen in the UK showing films especially made for this format, sometimes in 3D, for which special glasses are supplied. IMAX cinemas are also in Trocadero at Piccadilly Circus and the Science Museum (see page 28).

1 Charlie Chaplin Walk, South Bank SE1
bfi.org.uk/incinemas/imax
- **T** 0870 787 2525
- ⊖ ⇌ Waterloo
- ✺ Daily 10–midnight; hours can vary
- ⑩ Cafe
- **£** Moderate

Coram's Fields

A children's park with a pet animal area which has sheep, goats, rabbits, guinea pigs, pigs, ducks, chickens and an aviary. Also an under-fives play area, paddling pool and drop-in centre, plus play area and sports ground for older children. No dogs, and no adults admitted without a child.

93 Guilford Street WC1
coramsfields.org
- **T** 020 7837 6138
- ✺ Easter–31 Oct 9–8;
  Nov–Easter 9–dusk
- ⊖ Russell Square
- ⑩ Cafe
- **£** Free

Funland

Indoor interactive entertainment park with simulator rides and video games.

Trocadero, Piccadilly Circus W1
londontrocadero.com
- **T** 020 7439 1914
- ✺ Sun–Thurs 10am–midnight,
  Fri and Sat 10am–1am
- **£** Free admission, then pay
  individually for rides and
  video games
- ⊖ Piccadilly Circus

HMS *Belfast*

Europe's last surviving big, armoured warship from World War II; clamber around gun turrets, bridge, hammock-slung mess decks and boiler room.

Morgan's Lane, Tooley Street SE1
hmsbelfast.iwm.org.uk
- **T** 020 7940 6300
- ✺ Daily, Mar–Oct 10–6;
  Nov–Feb 10–5
- ⊖ ⇌ London Bridge
- ⑩ Cafe
- **£** Moderate

Horse Guards Parade: Changing the Guard

The mounted ceremony by the Household Cavalry. Changing the Guard also at Buckingham Palace (see page 10).

Whitehall SW1
- ✹ Mon–Sat 11am; Sun 10am
- ⊖ Westminster, Embankment or Charing Cross.
- ⇌ Charing Cross

Little Angel Theatre

Famous puppet theatre.

14 Dagmar Passage (off Cross Street), Islington N1
littleangeltheatre.com
- T 020 7226 1787
  Telephone for times of performances.
  Advance booking necessary
- ⊖ Angel or Highbury & Islington.
- ⇌ Essex Road

London Aquarium

An aquatic spectacular.

County Hall, Riverside Building, Westminster Bridge Road SE1
londonaquarium.co.uk
- T 020 7967 8000
- ✹ Daily 10–6 (last admission 5)
- ⊖ Westminster or Waterloo
- ⦿⊙ Cafe
- £ Expensive

The London Dungeon

Horror museum with state-of-the-art effects depicting torture and death in spine-chilling detail, including 'Sentenced to Death' boat-ride experience.

23–34 Tooley Street SE1
thedungeons.com
- T 020 7403 7221
- ✹ Apr–Sept 10–6 (July–Aug, Mon–Wed 10–9, but telephone for confirmation); Oct–Mar 10–5
- ⊖ London Bridge

Museum of London

Built on the West Gate of London's Roman fort, this is the best way to meander through London's 2,000-year history, pausing to see a Roman shoe, the Lord Mayor's State Coach or a Victorian shop counter. In every room it is Londoners who are telling the story, whether through their Roman storage jars, their Tudor leather clothes or their Suffragette posters.

150 London Wall EC2
museumoflondon.org.uk
- T 0870 444 3852
- ✹ Mon–Sat 10–5.50; Sun noon–5.50
- ⊖ Barbican, Moorgate or St Paul's
- ⇌ Moorgate, Liverpool Street or City Thameslink
- ⦿⊙ Restaurant
- £ Free

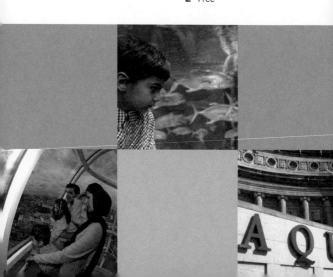

Families and kids

London's Transport Museum

CLOSED until autumn 2007

Tells the story of the world's largest urban public transport system, which covers more than 5,000 miles (8,047km) and moves millions of people around the city each day. There are buttons to push and plenty of vehicles. Star attractions include the Underground simulator.

39 Wellington Street, Covent Garden Piazza WC2

www.ltmuseum.co.uk

- **T** 020 7379 6344
- ⊖ Covent Garden
- ⇌ Charing Cross
- ✵ Daily 10–6 (Fri 11–6)
- ⦿ Cafe
- £ Moderate

The Original London Sightseeing Tour

Cruise about town on an open-top double-decker bus, whose six routes cover 80 stops; tickets and route maps available on board.

Pick-up points include Victoria Street, Haymarket, Marble Arch, Strand and Charing Cross Pier

theoriginaltour.com

- **T** 020 8877 1722
- ✵ Daily 8.30–6; departures approximately every 10 minutes
- £ Very expensive

Ticket valid for 24 hours

River trips

Great fun and a good way to catch some of the best views of London from the Thames. Central London piers at Westminster, Charing Cross and the Tower of London. Boats sail from these eastwards (downstream) to Greenwich, Docklands and the Thames Barrier, and westwards (from Westminster pier only) to Hampton Court, Richmond and Kew.

See citycruises.com, wpsa.co.uk and bateauxlondon.com for further information.

V&A Museum of Childhood

This enormous train shed is packed with Noah's Arks, toy soldiers and even a model circus. It has re-opened with a smashing new front entrance and gallery, a state-of-the-art learning centre and a programme of exhibitions and events.

Cambridge Heath Road E2

vam.ac.uk/moc

- **T** 020 8983 5200
- ✵ Daily 10–5.45
- ⊖ ⇌ Bethnal Green
- ⦿ Cafe
- £ Free

⚡ Cinemas

There are many cinemas in the West End showing first-run mainstream films, especially in Leicester Square. Prince Charles Cinema (0870 811 2559), just off Leicester Square, has very cheap tickets for almost-new films. There are also arthouse cinemas showing less commercial and subtitled films. The three-screen National Film Theatre (020 7928 3232) on the South Bank shows new and classic movies, including themed seasons. There are huge IMAX-screen cinemas at the South Bank, Trocadero and Science Museum (see Families and kids, pages 72–77). The annual London Film Festival takes place in October/November.

⚡ Theatre

Information

Time Out, London's weekly entertainment guide, has the most comprehensive theatre listings and reviews. Information can also be found in *What's On in London* magazine, the *Evening Standard* and national newspapers. See too the *What's On Stage* website: www.whatsonstage.com

Tickets

You can usually buy tickets direct from the theatres (by phone or in person) or from ticket agencies, which charge a booking fee (e.g. Ticketmaster 0870 534 4444, Keith Prowse Ticketing 0870 840 1111). At TKTS in Leicester Square WC2 there are a limited number of half-price tickets (plus a £2 service charge) for some West End shows available on the day of performance.

West End theatre

There are a huge range of musicals, drama, comedy and thrillers on offer in central London, especially in Shaftesbury Avenue, Charing Cross Road, St Martin's Lane and Soho. The Royal National Theatre on the South Bank (020 7452 3000) puts on the best of British, international, classic and modern drama on three stages: the Olivier, Lyttleton and Cottesloe. The Barbican Centre stages a wide range of international drama throughout the year in the large Barbican Theatre and a small studio theatre, The Pit. The Royal Shakespeare Company (0870 609 1110), which specialises in staging the plays of William Shakespeare and his contemporaries, as well as other drama, has a London season each year.

Off-West End theatre

Look in the listings for the Almeida, Bush, Donmar Warehouse, Gate, Hampstead, Lyric Hammersmith, Riverside Studios and the Royal Court, where the theatres tend to be smaller and the shows more varied than in the West End.

Fringe and pub theatre

Fringe provides an 'alternative' theatre experience in about 50 small venues all over London, which are often pub theatres such as the Etcetera, Finborough, Jermyn Street Theatre, New End and Southwark Playhouse.

⚡ Comedy

The Comedy Store, Jongleurs and Banana Cabaret are just a few of the dozens of comedy clubs in London's thriving comedy scene, although the best-known comedians often appear in West End theatres too.

musicals, dramas, comedy and thrillers

© BTA (trading as visit**Britain**) 2005.

For information and ticket bookings

London Pass
0870 242 9988
www.londonpass.com

London Theatre Bookings
020 7851 0300
www.londontheatrebookings.com

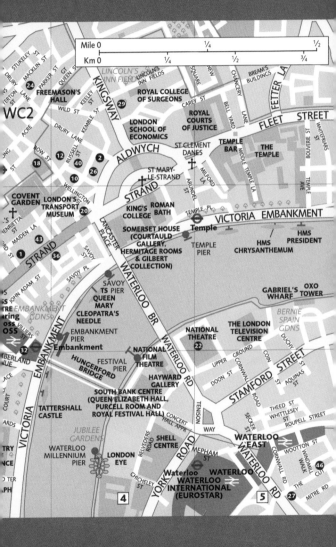

see overleaf for key

Central London

Hammersmith

Victoria

Barbican

⭐ Classical music, opera and dance

Classical music
The major classical music festival is the annual Henry Wood Promenade Concerts, known as the Proms, at the Royal Albert Hall during the summer. Other festivals include City of London, Spitalfields and outdoor concerts at Kenwood Lake on Hampstead Heath in the summer. London has five major full-size orchestras, plus many top-quality smaller orchestras.

Opera
Grand international opera can be seen at the Royal Opera House and English National Opera, Coliseum (performed in English). There is open-air opera at Holland Park in the summer.

Dance
The Royal Ballet is at the Royal Opera House in Covent Garden, and there is also ballet at the Coliseum and Sadler's Wells, with other forms of dance at the Peacock Theatre. Dance Umbrella, a world showcase for contemporary dance, takes place in Sept–Nov.

⭐ Jazz and blues
Venues include Ronnie Scott's, Jazz Cafe, 100 Club, Pizza on the Park and Pizza Express, Soho.

⭐ Rock and pop
Venues include Wembley Arena, Earl's Court, Shepherd's Bush Empire, Brixton Academy, Hammersmith Apollo and the Astoria.

⭐ Major venues

Barbican Concert Hall
Barbican Centre, Silk Street EC2
barbican.org.uk
T   020 7638 8891
⊖ Barbican or Moorgate

English National Opera, Coliseum
St Martin's Lane WC2
eno.org
T   0870 145 0200
⊖ Leicester Square, Charing Cross, Embankment or Covent Garden

Royal Albert Hall
Kensington Gore SW7
royalalberthall.com
T   020 7589 8212
⊖ South Kensington

Royal Opera House
Covent Garden WC2
royalopera.org
T   020 7304 4000
⊖ Covent Garden

Sadler's Wells Theatre
Rosebery Avenue EC1
sadlerswells.com
T   0870 737 7737
⊖ Angel

South Bank Centre
(inc. Royal Festival Hall, Queen Elizabeth Hall and Purcell Room)

South Bank SE1
southbankcentre.org.uk
T   08703 800 400
⊖ Waterloo

⚜ The Clubbing Scene

Often considered as one of the world's 'coolest' cities, it is no surprise that London boasts a cutting-edge clubbing scene. Among the variety of offerings, many of the city's clubs have gained worldwide acclaim. Some of the best are listed below.

The End & AKA

18 West Central Street, WC1A 1JJ
www.endclub.com

T 020 7419 9199,

⚜ Tue-Fri 6–3, Sat 7–6, Sun 10–4

£ £3-15

+ Euro, breakbeat, house, techno, trance

⊖ Tottenham Court Road or Holborn

Along with its sister club AKA, the End is one of London's top venues, boasting an "island" DJ booth in the main room. Sleek and very stylish, the End hosts a wide range of DJ acts six nights a week.

Fabric

77a Charterhouse Street, EC1M 6H
www.fabriclondon.com

T 020 7336 8898

⚜ Fri-Sat 10–close

£ £10-20

+ Euro, drum 'n bass, house, techno, trance, breakbeat

⊖ Farringdon

One of London's big-hitters in clubland, with an ear-defying sound system, cutting-edge music, impressive light shows and space for 1500 to let loose all at the same time.

Heaven

11 The Arches,
Villiers Street, WC2N 6NG
www.heaven-london.com

T 020 7930 2020

⚜ Mon, Wed 10.30–3, Fri-Sat 10.30–5

£ £6-15

+ Euro, house, techno, trance

⊖ Charing Cross or Embankment

Another of London's great clubs – th one probably the best-known gay nightclub in the world. The cavernou main room, ringed by pedestals, is packed most nights of the week. Out back are smaller more intimate spaces, while the VIP room boasts velvet seats and fish tanks.

cutting-
edge
clubbing
scene

Credit: The End

Credit: Fabric

Herbal

12-14 Kingsland Road

www.herbaluk.com

T 020 7613 4462

✳ Tue-Sun 6–close

£ £5-12

+ Euro, house, techno, trance, Urban

⊖ Shoreditch/Old Street/Liverpool Street

Set in a converted warehouse in the trend-setting neighbourhood of Hoxton, Herbal lays on a little something for every taste, with smallish, intimate rooms spanning three floors.

Ministry of Sound

103 Gaunt Street, SE1 6DP

www.ministryofsound.com

T 020 7378 6528

✳ Wed 9–6, Fri 10–6, Sat midnight–10

+ Alternative rock, euro, house, techno, Top 40 chart, trance

£ £5-15

⊖ Elephant & Castle

Arguably the biggest, most influential nightclub in the world, spawning a brand name which has become synonymous with great dance music. Ministry of Sound established itself as one of London's best-known dance venues during the 1990s and still attracts superstar DJs.

Scala

278 Pentonville Road

www.scala-london.co.uk

T 020 7833 2022

✳ Mon, Thurs 9–3; Fri-Sat 9–5

+ House, techno, trance, hip-hop

£ £6–15

⊖ King's Cross

A live music venue during the week, Scala transforms itself into a hip club at weekends, with a range of garage, funky house, trance and hip-hop. There are various mezzanine levels offering views over the stage. Also boasts one of London's best sound systems.

Credit: Fabric

garage, funky house, trance, hip-hop

Credit: Fabric

🔲 Shopping areas

Bond Street

Mixes haute-couture outlets with art galleries. Asprey, one of the world's great luxury stores, is here, as is the Fine Art Society. Parallel to Bond Street is Savile Row, famous for gentlemen's tailoring.

Mayfair W1

⊖ Bond Street or Green Park

Charing Cross Road

A name synonymous with bookshops and books, both new and second-hand, from large concerns such as Foyles and Blackwell's, to specialist shops such as Murder One (crime, horror, fantasy and romance) and Zwemmer Media Arts (photography and cinema).

Soho WC2

⊖ Leicester Square

Oxford Street

The capital's main shopping artery includes Marks & Spencer, Selfridges, John Lewis, branches of most significant chains and large record shops.

Mayfair/Marylebone W1

⊖ Oxford Circus, Bond Street, Marble Arch or Tottenham Court Road

Regent Street

John Nash's elegantly curving street has shops such as Mappin & Webb (silver), Liberty, Hamleys, Laura Ashley, Austin Reed and the Disney Store.

Mayfair/Soho W1

⊖ Piccadilly Circus or Oxford Circus

Tottenham Court Road

Well known for its choice of home and electrical stores, such as Heal's (furniture) and HI-FI Experience (hi-fi).

Bloomsbury W1

⊖ Tottenham Court Road

🔲 Department stores

Fortnum & Mason

Before going in, do not miss the clock, with Messrs Fortnum and Mason bowing to each other on the hour. Prices are high, but the shop-brand goods make great presents.

181 Piccadilly W1

T 020 7734 8040

⊖ Piccadilly Circus or Green Park

Hamleys

An eternal favourite with children (and adults), it is packed with toys and games. High prices.

188–196 Regent Street W1

T 0800 2802 444

⊖ Oxford Circus

Harrods

Vast emporium contains almost anything you might be looking for, and 19 places to eat. The food halls are spectacular.

Knightsbridge SW1

T 020 7730 1234

⊖ Knightsbridge

Harvey Nichols

London's classiest clothes shop, from its window displays to fashion floors.

109–125 Knightsbridge SW1

T 020 7235 5000

⊖ Knightsbridge

Liberty

From sumptuous fabrics to china and glass, it mixes high fashion with Arts and Crafts heritage.

Regent Street W1

T 020 7734 1234

⊖ Oxford Circus

🔲 Food and drink

Carluccio's
A designer deli selling only the most refined goods, such as truffle oil, black pasta and balsamic vinegar.
28a Neal Street WC2
T 020 7240 1487
⊖ Covent Garden

Fresh & Wild
Organic foods, plus ready-to-eat preparations and a juice bar. Five other London branches.
49 Parkway Road NW1
T 020 7428 7575
⊖ Camden Town

Neal's Yard Dairy
More than 50 varieties of British cheese ripened to perfection.
17 Shorts Gardens WC2
T 020 7240 5700
⊖ Covent Garden or Leicester Square

Royal Mile Whiskies
As well as wine, has more than 170 Scottish malt whiskies in stock.
3 Bloomsbury Street WC1
T 020 7436 4763
⊖ Tottenham Court Road

R Twining & Co
This little, atmospheric shop was where the tea merchant set up his business in 1706.
216 Strand WC2
T 020 7353 3511
⊖ Temple

Vinopolis
Mouthwatering breads, cheeses, olives and, of course, wines in a shop adjoining the wine tour. Also a wine bar and restaurant.
Bank End SE1
T 020 7940 8311
⊖ ⇌ London Bridge

🔲 Street markets

Borough Market
Best of British produce. Meat, cheese, fruit and vegetables.
Corner of Borough High Street and Stoney Street SE1
❋ Fri 12–6; Sat 9–4
⊖ ⇌ London Bridge

Brixton Market
Popular with the local African-Caribbean community for buying such food as mangoes, sweet potatoes, snapper fish, calf's feet and ready-cooked delicacies.
Brixton Station Road, Electric Avenue and Popes Road SW9
❋ Mon, Tues, Thurs–Sat 8–6; Wed 8–3
⊖ ⇌ Brixton

Camden Markets
Extend all the way from the Underground station to Camden Lock. Clothes, crafts and fruit and vegetables.
Camden High Street to Chalk Farm Road NW1
❋ Most markets daily 10–6
⊖ Camden Town

Petticoat Lane Market
Bargain hard for fashion, leather, household goods and knick-knacks.
Middlesex Street E1
❋ Mon–Fri and Sun 9–2
⊖ Aldgate or Aldgate East

Portobello Market

All kinds of stuff available. Lower prices further down the hill.

Portobello Road W11

❀ General: Mon–Wed, Fri 8–6.30;
Thurs 8–1; Sat 8–6.30
Antiques: Sat 6–6
Bric-a-brac: Fri, Sat 8–5

⊖ Ladbroke Grove

Spitalfields Market

Craft market, clothing, accessories and organic food in an historic building.

Commercial Street E1

❀ General: Mon–Fri 11–3, Sun 10–5
Organic stalls Fri, Sun 10–5

⊖ ⇌ Liverpool Street

◩ Art and antiques

Bonham's

The strength of this auction house lies in its 20th-century and specialist sales. Less expensive goods are sold in its Chelsea galleries.

101 New Bond Street W1

T 020 7447 7447

⊖ Sloane Square

Christie's

International auction house with departments ranging from grand old masters to tribal art. A second, less expensive sale room is in South Kensington.

8 King Street SW1

T 020 7839 9060

⊖ Green Park

Sotheby's

The world's largest auction house with a huge number of sale rooms for all kinds of objects.

34–35 New Bond Street W1

T 020 7293 5000

⊖ Bond Street

TELEPHONE

London Calling

Eating and drinking

Eating out in London can be a wonderful experience. As you'd expect in a world city, you can find the food of almost any country here. Prices vary enormously. Pubs and cafes tend to be cheaper than restaurants and hotels. The following places to eat are graded £, ££ or £££ in rising order of cost.

⭐ Cafes and pubs

Bush Garden Café (£)
Homely wholefood cafe with garden, complete with rain canopy and children's playhouse.

59 Goldhawk Road W12
T 020 8743 6372
⊖ Goldhawk Road

Paul (£)
Both Parisian in style yet informal, this cafe and shop offers exquisite hot snacks and pâtisserie. Other branches in London.

29 Bedford Street WC2
T 020 7836 3304
⊖ Covent Garden

Cow (£)
A superb, intimate gastro-pub with traditional pub decor and a hip yet friendly clientele. Seafood is a speciality here.

89 Westbourne Park Road W2
T 020 7221 0021
⊖ Royal Oak, Westbourne Park

Giraffe (£)
Very popular with families, a popular chain offering an eclectic menu to suit all tastes and budgets. Expect queues during the weekend. Other branches in London.

6–8 Blandford Street W1
T 020 7935 2333
⊖ Baker Street

⭐ British

St John (££)
This is a carnivore's delight, with such dishes as pig's trotters and offal, served by one of London's top chefs. The puddings are also a delight and quintessentially British.

26 St John Street EC1
T 020 7251 0848
⊖ Farringdon

Inn the Park (£–££)
A striking new Oliver Peyton venture, with seasonal British dishes and an all-day cafe menu. Check out the turfed roof!

St James's Park SW1
T 020 7451 9999
⊖ Green Park, Piccadilly

Lindsay House (£££)
Modern British cuisine cooked to perfection by the renowned Richard Corrigan in elegant, pared-down surroundings, in the heart of Soho.

21 Romilly Street W1
T 020 7439 0450
⊖ Leicester Square

Dorchester Grill Room (£££)
A gloriously grand setting with tapestries on the walls. Classic British dishes are brought to the table under silver cloches.

The Dorchester, 53 Park Lane W1
T 020 7317 6336
⊖ Hyde Park Corner

Eating and drinking

🗺 European

The Wolseley (££)
One of London's prized new dining spots set in an old car showroom, with an art-deco interior and an eclectic day and evening menu.

160 Piccadilly W1
T 020 7499 6996
T Green Park

The Ledbury (££)
An award-winning new Notting Hill restaurant (with one Michelin star) offering superb French cuisine. Booking essential.

127 Ledbury Road W11
T 020 7792 9090
⊖ Westbourne Park

Sardo (£)
Good-value eaterie, with simple but well-executed dishes. Many of the ingredients and wines are sourced directly from Sardinia.

45 Grafton Way W1
T 020 7387 2521
⊖ Warren Street

The River Café (£££)
A fantastic setting, with outside tables overlooking the Thames, this famous hotspot is expensive but it is well worth it. Booking essential.

Thames Wharf, Rainville Road W6
T 020 7386 4200
⊖ Hammersmith

Club Gascon (£££)
Renowned for its foie gras, this is a plush and pricey venue, but the food is imaginative and the menu is divided into five sections – perfect for the gourmand. Booking essential.

57 West Smithfield Street EC1
T 020 7796 0600
⊖ Barbican, Farringdon

Fino (££)
Stylish and spacious Spanish restaurant and bar, which serves delectable tapas from an extensive and varied menu. The desserts are to die for, too.

33 Charlotte Street W1
T 020 7813 8010
⊖ Goodge Street,
    Tottenham Court Road

Café Corfu (£)
A London stalwart, serving Greek cuisine, with deliciously spiced dishes and an excellent wine list. Belly dancers and DJs at the weekend.

7 Pratt Street NW1
T 020 7267 8088
⊖ Camden Town,
    Mornington Crescent

Moro (££)
With a top-selling cookbook and a forever packed restaurant, Moro's success lies in its modern interpretation of Spanish and North African cuisine. Booking essential.

34–36 Exmouth Market EC1
T 020 7833 8336
⊖ Farringdon

a fantastic setting .... well worth it

🍱 Asian

Hakkasan (£££)

Fine, pricey Chinese fare in extremely sophisticated surroundings. The dim sum are unrivalled and worth sampling at lunchtime. Booking for dinner is advisable.

8 Hanway Place W1
T 020 7907 1888
⊖ Tottenham Court Road

Sekara (£)

This Sri Lankan diner provides a laid-back bistro setting and good-value fare. Many fish dishes on offer, and some spicy ones, so beware!

3 Lower Grosvenor Place SW1
T 020 7834 0722
⊖ Victoria

New Tayyab (£)

A prime tourist attraction, with standard curry-house fare. Worth it for the experience, with Bollywood hits blasting out and trendy young things being boisterous.

83 Fieldgate Street E1
T 020 7247 9543
⊖ Aldgate East, Whitechapel

Yo! Sushi (£–££)

The original Yo! has had a re-fit. It now offers colour-coded plates of sushi, which you pick from a *kaiten* (double-track conveyor belt). An unusual eating experience.

52 Poland Street W1
T 020 7287 0443
⊖ Oxford Circus

Café Spice Namaste (££)

Pan-Indian cuisine, with such dishes as venison and duck tikka, and homemade chutneys. Dine al fresco in the new Ginger Garden, and enjoy the outside *tandoor* (barbecue).

16 Prescot Street E1
T 020 7488 9242
⊖ Aldgate, Tower Hill

E&O (££)

Very hip and stylish, E & O is always packed, and it is perfect for celebrity-spotting. It is a varied Asian menu, with divine dim sum being its speciality. Booking essential at weekends.

14 Blenheim Crescent W11
T 020 7229 5454
⊖ Ladbroke Grove, Notting Hill Gate

Busaba Eathai (£)

With shared tables, bench-seating and a no-booking policy, this is good-quality and reasonable Thai cuisine in a contemporary setting.

22 Store Street WC1
T 020 7299 7900
⊖ Goodge Street,
   Tottenham Court Road

Amaya (£££)

One of London's top-end Indian restaurants with an opulent setting, its speciality is kebabs and also desserts to die for.

Halkin Arcade SW1
T 020 7823 1166
⊖ Knightsbridge

perfect for celebrity-spotting

Zuma (£££)

Competing with Nobu as the capital's most glamorous Japanese dining spot, it is worth booking weeks before arriving in London. The food is impeccable and the menu extensive.

5 Raphael Street SW7

T 020 7584 1010

⊖ Knightsbridge

🔀 Fish and Vegetarian

Manna (£)

Unpretentious vegetarian restaurant close to Primrose Hill, serving international dishes (such as Indian or Mediterranean). Try the organic ice creams to finish.

4 Erskine Road NW3

T 020 78028

⊖ Chalk Farm

Blah Blah Blah (£)

Some of the best vegetarian fare in London in a lilac-hued, romantic setting. With a global menu, leaning towards Japanese and Asian flavours, this is a venue not to miss.

78 Goldhawk Road W12

T 020 8746 1337

⊖ Goldhawk Road

FishWorks (££)

There is a fishmonger at the front and a two-level restaurant behind, with an attractive canopied garden. Booking essential at weekends.

6 Turnham Green Terrace W4

T 020 8994 0086

Fish Hoek (££)

Named after a seaside suburb of Cape Town, it specialises in South African fish dishes. It can get very crowded at the weekends (with two fixed sittings), but the food is well worth it.

8 Elliott Road W4

T 020 8742 0766

⊖ Turnham Green

Brady's (£)

A unique, eccentric atmosphere at this fish and chip restaurant. The starters are excellent, with potted shrimps, dressed crab and salmon fish cakes.

513 Old York Road SW18

T 020 8877 9599

⇌ Wandsworth Town

Overseas offices

AUSTRIA
Britain Visitor Centre
c/o British Council
Siebensterngassee 21
1070 Wien
T: 0800-150 170 (gebührenfrei)
F: 01-533 26 16 85
E: a-info@visitbritain.org
W: www.visitbritain.com/at

AUSTRALIA:
VisitBritain
Level 2
15 Blue Street
North Sydney, NSW 2060
Public and Trade Enquiries: 1300 85 85 89
T: +61 (0)2 9021 4400
F +61 (0)2 9021 4499
E: visitbritainaus@visitbritain.org
W: www.visitbritain.com.au

BRUSSELS:
VisitBritain
Brand Whitlocklaan 87 Bd Brand Whitlock
Brussel 1200 Bruxelles
T: + 32 2 646 35 10
F: +32 2 646 39 86
E: british.be@visitbritain.org
W: www.visitbritain.com/be (Flemish)
W: www.visitbritain.com/be2 (French)

BRAZIL
VisitBritain
Centro brasileiro britanico
Rua ferreira de araujo 741, 1 andar
Pinheiros
Sao paulo
Sp 05428-002
Brazil
T: +(55) 11 3245 7650
F: +(55) 11 3245 7651
E: brasil@visitbritain.org
W: www.visitbritain.com/br

CANADA:
VisitBritain
5915 Airport Road, Suite 120
Mississauga, Ontario L4V 1T1
T: 1 888 VISIT UK or +1 905 405 1720
F: + 1 905 405 1835
E: britinfo@visitbritain.org
W: www.visitbritain.com/ca

CHINA:
VisitBritain
c/o Cultural and Education Section
British Embassy
4/F Landmark Building Tower 1
8 North Dongsanhuan Road
Chaoyang District
100004, Beijing
China
T: + (8610) 6590 6903 Ext 209
F: + (8610) 6590 0977
VisitBritain
c/o British Consulate General Shanghai
1st Floor Cross Tower
318 Fu Zhou Lu
200001, Shanghai
China
T: + (8621) 6391 2626
F: + (8621) 6391 2121

CZECH REPUBLIC:
VisitBritain
c/o British Council
Bredovsky dvur
Politickych veznu 13,
110 00 Prague
Czech Republic
T: +42 0 221 991 178
F: British Council fax 00 42 0 224 933 847

DENMARK:
VisitBritain
Kristianiagade 8, 3.
2100 Copenhagen
T: + 45 70 21 50 11
F: + 45 33 75 50 08
E: dkweb@visitbritain.org
W: www.visitbritain.com/dk

FRANCE:
VisitBritain
22, Avenue Franklin Roosevelt
75008, Paris
France
Office de Tourisme de Grande-Bretagne
(Postal address)
BP 154-08
75363 Paris Cedex 08
T: + 33 1 58 36 50 50
F: + 33 1 58 36 50 51
E: gbinfo@visitbritain.org
W: www.visitbritain.com/fr (en français)

GERMANY
VisitBritain & Britain Visitor Centre
Hackescher Markt 1
10178 Berlin
T: +49 30 315 7190
F: +49 30 315 7190
E: gb-info@visitbritain.org
W: www.visitbritain.com/de

GREECE
VisitBritain
29 Michalakopoulou St.
Athens, 11528
Direct Tel:+30 210 7240349
Direct Fax:+30 210 7240319
Switchboard:+30 210 7245541- 210 7210774

HONG KONG:
7/F British Council
3 Supreme Court Road
Admiralty
Hong Kong
T: + (852) 3515 7815
F: + (852) 3515 7800
E: hongkong@visitbritain.org
W: www.visitbritain.com/hk

HUNGARY
Szadai ut 11
Veresegyhaz 2112
Hungary
T: +36 28 386 632
F: +36 28 386 623

INDIA:
VisitBritain
202 - 203 JMD Regent Square, 2nd Floor
Mehrauli Gurgaon Road
Gurgaon - 122 001 (Haryana)
India
Tel : 00-91-124-4103281- 84.
Fax : 00-91-124-4103280.
E: india@visitbritain.org
W: www.visitbritain.com/in

IRELAND:
VisitBritain
Newmount House
22-24 Lower Mount Street
Dublin 2
T: + 353 1 670 8000
F: + 353 1 670 8244
E: contactus@visitbritain.org
W: www.visitbritain.ie

ITALY
VisitBritain
Ente Nazionale Britannico per il Turismo
Corso Magenta 32
20123 Milano
T: +39 02 88 08 151
F: +39 02 7201 0086
E: informazioni@visitbritain.org
W: www.visitbritain.com/ciao

JAPAN:
VisitBritain
Akasaka Twin Tower 1F
2-17-22 Akasaka
Minato-ku
Tokyo 107-0052
T: +81 3 5562 2550
F: +81 3 5562 2551
E: japan@visitbritain.org
W: www.visitbritain.com/jp (Japanese)
W: www.uknow.or.jp (Japanese/English)

MALAYSIA
VisitBritain
c/o British Council
Ground Floor, West Block
Wisma Selangor Dredging
142C Jalan Ampang
50450 Kuala Lumpur
Malaysia
T: + 60 (0)3 2723 7970
F: + 60 (0)3 2713 6599
email: sumathi.ramanathan@visitbritain.org

NETHERLANDS
VisitBritain
Prins Hendrikkade 186-187
1011 TD Amsterdam
Or postal:
Postbus 20650, 1001 NR, Amsterdam
T: +31 20 689 0002
F: +31 20 689 0003
E: nl@visitbritain.org
W: www.visitbritain.com/nl

NEW ZEALAND:
VisitBritain
c/o British Consulate-General Office
Level 17, IAG House
151 Queen Street
PO Box 105-652
Auckland
Public and Trade Enquiries: 0800 700 741
T: +64 (0)9 309 1899
F: +64 (0)9 377 6965
E: newzealand@visitbritain.org
W: www.visitbritain.co.nz

NORWAY
Visitors:
VisitBritain
Olav V's gate 5
0161 Oslo
Post:
Det Britiske turistkontor
PB 1554 Vika
0117 Oslo
T: + 47 22 01 20 80 (call centre)
F: + 47 22 01 20 84
E: norge@visitbritain.org (call centre mail)
W: www.visitbritain.com/no

PORTUGAL:

VisitBritain Portugal
Largo Rafael Bordalo Pinheiro, nº 16
2º piso, sala 210
1200-396 Lisboa
Tel: 00351 21 3240190
Fax: 00351 21 3240191
W: www.visitbritain.com/pt

RUSSIA:

British Council
VGBIL
Nikoloyamskaya, 1
Moscow 109189
Russia
T: + 7 (095) 782 0200
F: + 7 (095) 124 7929
W: www.visitbritain.com/ru

SINGAPORE:

VisitBritain
600 North Bridge Road
#09-10 Parkview Square
Singapore 188778
T: +(65) 6511 4311
F: +(65) 6511 4300
E: singapore@visitbritain.org
W: www.visitbritain.com/sg

SOUTH AFRICA:

VisitBritain
Lancaster Gate
Hyde Park Lane
Hyde Lane
Hyde Park, Sandton 2196
PO Box 41896, (postal address)
Craighall 2024
T: +27 11 325 0591
E: johannesburg@visitbritain.org
W: www.visitbritain.com/za

SOUTH KOREA:

British Embassy
Taepyeongno 40
4 Jeong-dong, Jung-gu
Seoul (100-120)
Korea
T: + 82 2 3210 5531
F: + 82 2 720 4928
W. www.visitbritain.com/kr

SPAIN:

Turismo Británico
Apartado de Correos 19205 (Post)
28080 Madrid
T: 902 171 181
E: turismo.britanico@visitbritain.org
W: www.visitbritain.com/es
C/ Caidos de la Division Azul, 20 (Office address)
28016 Madrid
T: +34 91.343.63.13.
F: +34 91.343.63.10.

SWEDEN

Brittiska Turistbyrån
Klara Norra Kyrkogata 29
Box 3102, 103 62 Stockholm
T: +46 8 4401 700
F: +46 8 21 31 29
E: info@brittiskaturistbyran.com
W: www.visitbritain.com/sverige
VisitBritain (postal address)
Box 3102, 103 62 Stockholm
T: 9 2512 2422
F: 00 468 21 31 29

THAILAND

VisitBritain
c/o British Council
254 Chulalongkorn Soi 64 Siam Square,
Phyathai Road Pathumwan,
Bangkok 10330
Thailand
Tel: +66-2-652-5480 Ext 115
Fax: +66-2-253-5312
E:pheeraphon.nonthasoot@visitbritain.org

UNITED ARAB EMIRATES:

VisitBritain
P O Box 33342
2nd Floor, Sharaf Building
Khalid Bin Waleed Road
Dubai, UAE
 T: +971 4 3979919
F: +971 4 3961884
E: dubai@visitbritain.org
W: www.visitbritain.com/me
<http://www.visitbritain.com/me>
(English language site)
W: www.visitbritain.com/ahlan
(Arabic language site)

USA:

VisitBritain
551 Fifth Avenue, Suite 701
New York, NY 10176-0799
T: + 1 800 462 2748
F: + 212 986 1188
E: travelinfo@visitbritain.org
W: www.visitbritain.com/usa
VisitBritain
625 N, Michigan Avenue
Suite 1001
Chicago 60611-1977
USA
T: + 312 787 0464
F: + 312 787 9641
VisitBritain
10880 Wilshire Blvd
Suite 570
Los Angeles 90024
T: + 310 470 2782
F: + 310 470 8549

Airports

Heathrow
T 0870 000 0123

Heathrow Express
from Paddington Station
T 0845 600 1515

Cost: £14.50 (£13.50 online) single/
£28.00 return

Time: allow 25 minutes maximum

Frequency: every 15 minutes from 5.10am

Tube
T 020 7222 1234

Cost: £4.00 single/
£8.00 return

Time: allow approximately 1 hour 15 minutes from Oxford Circus

Coach
National Express
T 08705 80 80 80

Heathrow Central Bus Station from Victoria Coach Station

Minimum direct journey time:
29 minutes

Maximum direct journey time:
1 hour 20 minutes

Maximum return fare: £11.00

Gatwick
T 0870 000 2468

Gatwick Express
from Victoria Station
T 0845 850 1530

Cost: £14.90 single/
£26.80 return

Time: allow 30 minutes

Frequency: every 15 minutes from approx. 3.30am

Tube
T 020 7222 1234

Cost: £3.00 from Oxford Circus to Victoria tube station

Time: allow 15 minutes maximum from Oxford Circus

Coach
National Express
T 08705 80 80 80

Gatwick South Terminal from Victoria Coach Station

Minimum direct journey time:
1 hour 5 minutes

Maximum direct journey time:
1 hour 50 minutes

Maximum return fare: £11.00

City Airport
T 020 7646 0088

Docklands Light Railway
T 020 7722 1234

Cost: £3 single from Canary Wharf tube station

Time: allow 10 to 15 minutes

Frequency: every 10 minutes from 6.13am

Tube
T 020 7222 1234

Cost: £3 single from Oxford Circus to London City Airport via DLR

Time: allow approximately 30 minutes from Oxford Circus

Rail and coach

National Rail Enquires
T 08457 48 49 50

All enquiries involving train times, costs and purchases to any UK destination from any London train station.

National Bus and Coach enquires
National Express **T** 08705 80 80 80
Stagecoach **T** 020 7122 1234

1 Charing Cross

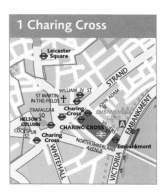

⇄ National Rail destinations: Kent, Hastings and south-east London.

⊖ Charing Cross for Bakerloo and Northern lines. Embankment for Bakerloo, Circle, District and Northern lines.

3 Marylebone

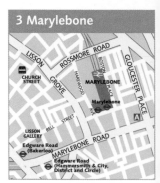

⇄ National Rail destinations: Aylesbury, High Wycombe, Bicester, Banbury, Leamington Spa, Stratford-upon-Avon, Birmingham (Snow Hill) and Kidderminster.

⊖ Bakerloo line.

2 Euston

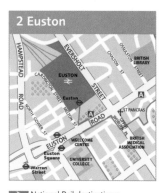

⇄ National Rail destinations: Birmingham, Manchester, Liverpool, Holyhead, Glasgow and local stopping services.

⊖ Euston for Victoria and Northern line City branch lines.

Euston Square for Circle, Hammersmith & City and Metropolitan lines.

4 Victoria

⇄ National Rail destinations: Kent, Surrey, Sussex, including Gatwick Airport and Brighton.

⊖ Victoria, District and Circle lines.

5 King's Cross & St Pancras

⇄ King's Cross National Rail destinations: Cambridge, King's Lynn, York, Durham, Newcastle, Edinburgh, Hull, North London, Hertfordshire, Bedfordshire and Peterborough.

⇄ St Pancras National Rail destinations: East Midlands, Yorkshire.

⊖ King's Cross St Pancras for Victoria, Northern, Piccadilly, Hammersmith & City, Circle and Metropolitan lines.

7 Paddington

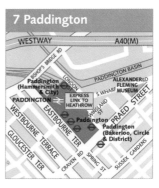

⇄ National Rail destinations: West Country, Bristol, Bath and South Wales, commuter services to West London and Thames Valley.

⊖ Hammersmith & City, Bakerloo, Circle and District.

6 Waterloo

⇄ National Rail destinations: south-west England.
⇄ Waterloo International: Eurostar trains to France and Belgium.
⇄ Waterloo East: Kent, trains coming from Charing Cross.

⊖ Bakerloo, Jubilee, Northern and Waterloo & City lines.

8 Liverpool Street

⇄ National Rail destinations: Stansted Airport, Cambridge, Lowestoft, Gt Yarmouth, Norwich, Ipswich, Colchester and Harwich. Suburban stations in north-east London.

⊖ Circle, Metropolitan, Hammersmith & City and Central.

Britain and London Visitor Centre

1 Regent Street,
London, England, SW1Y 4XT
E-mail blvcinfo@visitbritain.org
Website www.visitbritain.com

Opening times
Summer season
Mon 09.30–6.30;
Tues–Fri 9–6.30;
Sat and Sun 10–4
Winter season
Mon 9.30–6.30
Tues–Fri 9–6.30
Sat and Sun 10–4

Waterloo

London Visitor Centre, Arrivals Hall,
Waterloo International Terminal, London,
England, SE1 7LT
T +44 (0)20 7620 1550
E-mail: london.visitorcentre@iceplc.com
Open daily 8.30am-10pm approx.

VisitBritain

Thames Tower, Blacks Road, London
W6 9EL, United Kingdom
www.visitbritain.com

Produced by Publishing at VisitBritain

Photography credits: britainonview.com/
Derek Forss/Pawel Libera/Doug McKi/
Eric Nathan/Adam Swaine; The End; Fabric;
London Zoo; London Wetland Centre/
Martin Senior; Madame Tussauds